Rent to Own

Other McGraw-Hill Books by Robert Irwin

Rent
TO
Own

Use Your Rent Money
to Get Started
Owning Real Estate

ROBERT IRWIN

McGraw-Hill

New York   Chicago   San Francisco   Lisbon   London   Madrid   Mexico City
Milan   New Delhi   San Juan   Seoul   Singapore   Sydney   Toronto

ISBN 13: 978-0-07-148829-7
ISBN 10: 0-07-148829-4

This publication is designed to provide accurate and authoritative information in regard to the subject matter covered. It is sold with the understanding that neither the author nor the publisher is engaged in rendering legal, accounting, futures/securities trading, or other professional service. If legal advice or other expert assistance is required, the services of a competent professional person should be sought.

——From a Declaration of Principles jointly adopted by a Committee
of the American Bar Association and a Committee of Publishers

McGraw-Hill books are available at special quantity discounts to use as premiums and sales promotions, or for use in corporate training programs. For more information, please write to the Director of Special Sales, Professional Publishing, McGraw-Hill, Two Penn Plaza, New York, NY 10121-2298. Or contact your local bookstore.

This book is printed on acid-free paper.

Contents

Preface

"If I could show you how to buy a home with your rent money, would you do it?"

That's not a rhetorical question. I was asking some friends of mine, a young couple, this very question not long ago. Their answer was something like this: "The market's slowing down, and prices are falling in some neighborhoods. I think we'll wait a little bit."

They felt that for them, the timing was wrong.

The trouble is that a few years ago when the market was going up in the double-digit range, I asked them the same question. And their reply was, "Prices are getting too high. We'll wait until the market cools off a bit."

In other words, the timing was *never* right to buy. Or to put it another way, it was always the right time to rent. When I pursued this issue with my friends, they mentioned, "Buying is hard! Renting is always easier and cheaper."

Unfortunately, nothing could be further from the truth. How *easy* is it when the landlord raises the rent? Or tells you that you have to move because the building is being sold or converted to condos or being torn down to build a strip mall? How easy is it when the landlord says "no pets" or demands you turn your stereo off at nine o'clock or refuses to give you new carpeting or to paint your kitchen and bedroom? There's nothing easy about not being able to control the future of where and how you'll live. And when you rent, you have virtually no control. (Even in a lease, at best you can control the rent for a year or so.)

And as for its being cheaper to rent than to own—it might be true in any given month. But what about over a year, 3 years, 5 years, 10 years? When you add up the costs of renting versus the costs of owning, you'll very quickly find that long-term price appreciation, equity return, and tax advantages make owning by far the cheaper way to go. As the chapters that follow will explain, that's the case for almost all markets and areas of the country.

Finally, just how hard is it to buy a home? High prices and a tightening of the mortgage market are, indeed, scaring many potential buyers. Yet, where there's a will, there's a way. One of the primary goals of this book is to show how you can use your rent money to obtain ownership.

As Will Rogers was fond of saying about real estate, "They ain't makin' any more of it!" Long term, almost no one has ever lost money when they bought property, even people who bought at the so-called worst of times.

And so I told my friends.

Skeptics though they might be, they listened. And they bought. And now that their former rent money is going to pay for their own home, they tell me they've never been happier.

Which is why I wrote this book. If you're a renter, it's time to stop, take a hard look at where your money is going, and reevaluate. I suspect you'll come to a better conclusion.

Why You Should Own Your Home

Rents are going up at the fastest rate in decades, all over the country.

Yet well over a third of all people in this country still rent instead of own a home. They rent in spite of the fact that the vast majority of renters actually *can* afford to buy a home (we'll see exactly how in the following chapters). If you are one of these renters, why don't you buy?

Could it be that you don't see the advantages of homeownership? After all, renters often point out that when something breaks in a rental, you just call the landlord to fix it (assuming, of course, you can get the landlord out to do the work in a reasonable amount of time!). But if you own your property, if anything breaks, you have to fix it yourself.

Further, many renters feel it's actually a lot cheaper to rent any given house, condo, or apartment than to buy it. So why not rent instead of buy?

Why Buy?

I remember an old poker player once telling me that if you ask people why they play, 99 percent of them will tell you it's for the fun of it. Yet every one of those people is unhappy unless they walk away from the game a winner, not a loser.

As a renter you may have all kinds of reasons for preferring to rent. But I would wager that 99 percent of renters would love to make a profit on their property. Of course, the bad thing about renting is that the renter can never make a profit—it all goes to the landlord. Owning is where the profits are. Those who invest in real estate are the ones who see their net worth grow over the years.

When you rent, the outcome is as certain as death and taxes—the rent always goes up, and you've got nothing to show for it at the end. Sure, during recessions landlords may not raise the rent for several years. But wait until the boom times come and you'll see those rental rates start hopping up and up, sometimes several times in a single year. (As this is being written, rents are skyrocketing in many parts of the country.)

When you own, it is quite likely that you will reap large profits. When times are good, people can significantly increase their home's value in just a few years. When times are very good, they can see prices appreciate in the double digits every year. (During the period between 2000 and 2006, some property owners saw their homes double in value!) The beauty of it, of course, is that even when times are bad, it's still possible to make a profit.

Is it really?

As the real estate market settles down (and declines in some areas of the country), talk always arises of whether it truly is better to own than to rent. Some in the media try to make the point that at certain points in the real estate cycle, it makes more sense to rent.

After all, if losses are occurring in the real estate market, doesn't renting make more sense? When you rent, you're never out more than your rental money each month. You don't have to worry about losing your equity, your down payment, or your shirt!

In this chapter we're going to look at how owners make a profit on their homes. (Unlike what many people suppose, it doesn't just depend on the market going up!) Then we'll compare renting with buying to see when and if one makes more sense than the other. Finally, we'll come up with an equation to help you determine whether buying or renting makes the most sense for you.

Where's the Profit?

A lot of people talk about making a profit by investing in property. But can you really do it, especially when the market's not superhot?

After all, today it's not cheap to buy a home. And prices in many areas have leveled off, and in others they've started to drift lower. Just like that woman on television who used to ask, where's the beef in the hamburger, where's the profit in owning real estate today?

It's a fair question. People who bought homes at the height of this last real estate boom saw the values of their property *decline* in just a few months once the boom went bust. During the 1990s, in the midst of the worst real estate recession since the Great Depression, property values declined as much as 30 percent in some areas in Southern California, parts of Florida, the Northeast, and other areas of the country. It's simply untrue that property always goes up in price. Sometimes it goes down. Where's the profit in that?

Here's where it is:

1. Leverage
2. Inflation
3. Equity return

Leverage

The Greek mathematician Archimedes (287 to 212 BC) is supposed to have said, "Give me a lever long enough and a fulcrum on which to place it and I will move the world." Leverage is everything. In an argument, if you've got leverage on your side, you're going to win. For example, a husband and wife are arguing about who should take out the garbage. He says with some justification that he's taken it out every day for the last month. They should share, and if they do, it's her turn. She simply smiles and blows him a kiss. Who do you think has the leverage and who's got the garbage?

Or you're pulled over for speeding. You argue with the officer that you were just keeping up with traffic, that road conditions are excellent, that you're driving a safe new car with new tires. Who do you think has leverage and who's got the ticket?

In real estate, *leverage* is what you, the buyer of a property, can use. And you can use it to make a profit almost anytime. Let's look at a basic example.

You buy a house on which you put $10,000 down, and the property goes from $100,000 to $110,000 in value (not an unrealistic amount given gains in recent years). What's your profit?

If you said 10 percent, you don't understand leverage. It's actually 100 percent. Fleshing out the example makes this clearer. You put down $10,000. The house then goes up in value $10,000. Your return on your original investment, at least on paper, is $10,000 or 100 percent.

Calculating Profit from Leverage

Down payment	$10,000
Price increase	10,000 (profit = 100 percent)
Your money doubles to	$20,000

Note: the property value does not need to go up 100 percent for you to make a 100 percent profit. Not even close.

Let's say the property you buy costs you $230,000 (close to the national average), and it goes up in value only $10,000 to $240,000. That's a price increase of only 4 percent.

However, if you had put $10,000 down, you would have then doubled your money while the house went up only a little over that 4 percent in value.

Calculating Profit from Price Increase

Purchase price	$230,000
Increase in value	10,000
Current price	$240,000

Percent increase in value of property: 4 percent
Percent profit: 100 percent

That's the power of leverage. In real estate you can put down very little of your own money when you buy. Purchasing a $230,000 house with $10,000 down (excluding closing costs—which is realistic because they can often be included in the mortgage or they can sometimes be paid by the seller) is not uncommon. Indeed, it's often the case that you can purchase the house with nothing down. Consider the leverage there!

This is one way of making other people's money work for you. In this case, it's the bank or other institutional lender who puts up 95 percent or more of the cash. We'll go into greater detail on how this is done in Chapter 6.

TIP

The important point to take home is that real estate offers you the opportunity to make *big* money from *little* money through leveraging the deal.

Now, let's take a look at inflation.

Inflation

Most of us think of inflation as a bad thing. Indeed, we constantly hear how the Federal Reserve is *fighting* inflation. One would think it's an enemy almost on par with a terrorist group.

That's far from the truth, however. Inflation can be either good or bad, depending on where you stand. It's actually a case of whose ox is being gored. If you're in a cash position and inflation eats away the value of your dollars, then you're sure to feel inflation is an evil monster. But if you own commodities, such as real estate properties, and inflation kicks up its value, then because of the leverage we were just looking at, inflation is your best friend.

How can inflation help you financially?

Let's consider the modest inflation we've had over the past few years—around 3 percent annually. (In the distant past, inflation has dropped to almost zero at times and soared into double digits at other times, so 3 percent is pretty low.) How can 3 percent inflation help you in real estate?

TRAP

The amazing price spikes in real estate during the period of 2002 to 2006 were not due mostly to high inflation but instead to strong demand for housing and a short supply.

It's important to understand what *inflation* actually is. It's the loss in value of our currency. Thus, 3 percent inflation means that the dollar buys 3 percent less than it used to. The same jar of jam that used to cost $1 would cost $1.03. The car that used to cost $20,000 would cost $20,600. And the house that used to cost $350,000 would cost $360,500. Note that the jar isn't any bigger, the car not any faster, and the house not improved. It's just that because money has lost value, it takes more of it to buy the same product.

Let's say that because of inflation, your house goes up by 3 percent, or $10,500. But that's not profit. After all, everything else, presumably, has also gone up by 3 percent so you're back to breaking even.

Not so. Remember leverage? Yes, the house cost $350,000, but you didn't put $350,000 into it. You put only, say, $10,000 into it.

Now, *based on the amount you invested*, you've made a stunning 105 percent return.

Calculating Profit from Inflation

Down payment	$10,000
Price increase	10,500 (profit = 105 percent)
Your money increases to	$20,500

TIP

What do you care if inflation has reduced the value of your money by 3 percent when it's given you a 105 percent profit!

Note that you made this money due to two factors. The first was that you leveraged the deal—that is, you put very little of your own money into it and used mostly other people's money (the bank's—see above). Second, inflation that just came naturally rolling along boosted the value of your property. Sure, it reduced the buying power of your money. But you made so much money, you don't care!

But, you say, you're a renter, not an owner. You're not locked into a long-term position, which ownership and mortgages can demand. You're free to roam (sort of like Don Quixote, who was fond of riding around the landscape tilting at windmills).

True, sort of. The thing is that ownership doesn't tie you down as much as you might imagine. In most cases an owner can sell, refinance, or rent (to someone like you) and get out from under the mortgage and the property.

What ownership does tie you down to is making oodles of money on a very small investment because of leverage and inflation.

And that freedom that renters have is the freedom to have the landlord raise the rent or throw you out for any reason with 30 to 60 days' notice. (With a lease, you may be locked in until the expiration of the lease, but typically that's only one year.) In other words, while the property owner is locked into profits, as a tenant, you're locked into . . . rent increases!

Equity Return

Finally, there's the matter of equity return on the mortgage. You don't hear much talk about this because it's generally overlooked. Yet it's an extremely powerful method of making money on property over time.

Equity return is simply what you get each month as you slowly pay down your mortgage. Some people use the term to mean the part of the mortgage payment that goes to principal, but a better way of looking at it is that it is the amount that is returned to your equity.

Think of it in terms of banking. Your home is your bank (in more ways than one). When you buy a home and get a mortgage, your home bank says, "$300,000 (for example) of your equity is now in a restricted account. It's there, but you can't touch it, for now. But each month as you make your payments, I'll take some of that payment (say $250 *or more*) out of that restricted account and put it into an open account that you can touch. After 30 years your restricted account will be down to zero balance. And your open account will have $300,000 in it." (See Table 1.1.)

Thus, each month a portion of your mortgage payment goes into that "open account." It's equity in your house that's returned to your use.

Keep in mind that this happens regardless of the influence of inflation or leverage. It's *in addition* to these. It's part of the structure of an *amortized loan*—that is, a loan that pays itself off. (Most loans are amortized.)

TRAP

If you buy a home with an interest-only mortgage, you have no equity return—which is another good reason to avoid this type of loan.

Further, the amount that goes to equity return usually increases each month as you pay off the mortgage. In our example, during the first year there may be around $250 a month of

TABLE 1.1 Mortgage Amortization Showing Equity Return on a $300,000 Fixed-Rate 30-Year Loan

	EQUITY RETURN	INTEREST	BALANCE OWED
Year 1	$3,047	$20,903	$296,952
Year 2	$3,267	$20,683	$293,684
Year 3	$3,503	$20,446	$290,180
Year 4	$3,757	$20,193	$286,423
Year 5	$4,028	$19,922	$282,394
Year 6	$4,320	$19,631	$278,074
Year 7	$4,632	$19,318	$273,442
Year 8	$4,967	$18,984	$268,475
Year 9	$5,326	$18,624	$263,148
Year 10	$5,711	$18,239	$257,437
Year 11	$6,124	$17,827	$251,312
Year 12	$6,567	$17,384	$244,745
Year 13	$7,042	$16,909	$237,703
Year 14	$7,551	$16,400	$230,152
Year 15	$8,097	$15,854	$222,056
Year 16	$8,682	$15,269	$213,373
Year 17	$9,309	$14,641	$204,064
Year 18	$9,983	$13,968	$194,082
Year 19	$10,704	$13,246	$183,376
Year 20	$11,478	$12,473	$171,898
Year 21	$12,307	$11,643	$159,590
Year 22	$13,197	$10,753	$146,393
Year 23	$14,152	$9,799	$132,242
Year 24	$15,175	$8,776	$117,066
Year 25	$16,271	$7,679	$100,795
Year 26	$17,448	$6,502	$83,347
Year 27	$18,709	$5,241	$64,637
Year 28	$20,061	$3,889	$44,575
Year 29	$21,512	$2,438	$23,063
Year 30	$23,064	$884	$0.00
Totals	$300,000	$418,524	$0.00

SUMMARY

Total equity return over 30 years = $300,000

equity return. But by the third year it's closer to $300 a month. By the tenth year it's $500 a month, and by the twenty-fifth year it's an amazing $1,500 per month. The magic is that each month more of your payment goes to return equity and less to interest. (This makes sense only because, as equity is returned, the mortgage balance goes down so there is less to pay interest on.)

TIP

The increase in equity return over time is one reason to avoid refinancing in the later years of a mortgage. Remember, with a new mortgage the equity return is much smaller. With an older mortgage, it's much bigger.

TRAP

The return of equity increases as described only if you've got an *amortized loan* that pays itself off over time. If you have an interest-only loan, as noted earlier, there will be no equity return. On an adjustable-rate loan, the equity return will vary depending on a variety of conditions. (See Chapter 6.)

Equity return is one of the great, unheralded advantages of homeownership. When you're paying rent, *all* of your payment goes to the landlord, and you never see any of it again. When you buy a home with a mortgage, a portion of each month's payment actually comes back to you. And, miracle of miracles, that portion gets bigger each month. If you buy a home with a $300,000 30-year fixed-rate mortgage on it, at the end of 30 years, you'll have $300,000 in equity—like cash in the bank. (That's in addition to what you've made through appreciation!) You don't have to do anything but make the payments. It's the ultimate no-brainer.

Further, at any time that you need cash, refinancing is available to get some or all of your equity back out. Thus, if you need money after, say, five years, you can take your returned equity out of the property in cash by refinancing. (Of course, if the value of your home has gone up during that time, you can take that out too.)

Sound too good to be true?

It's not. And it helps explain why homeownership is better for most people than any other possible investment—from stocks to bonds and from gold to diamonds.

Tax and Interest Deductions

But all of this requires you to make monthly payments—often *big* monthly payments. As a renter, you may have heard that when you buy, your payments will be higher than your rent. For example, the very same house that rents for $1,500 a month might cost you $2,500 monthly in principal, interest, taxes, and insurance to buy. If that's so, how can you justify the extra $1,000 a month a purchase might require?

Doesn't it make sense to simply rent? Don't the higher monthly payments nullify all the advantages of leverage, inflation, and equity return just described?

No, not usually. There are other factors, mainly the largesse of the United States through tax advantages offered to owners. The government allows taxpayers to deduct a substantial amount of their mortgage interest (up to a million-dollar mortgage as of this writing) from their ordinary income. You can also deduct your state property taxes from your ordinary income when calculating your tax. Thus your monthly payment is, in effect, subsidized by the federal and state governments.

TIP

Tax rules are complex. The simplified examples and rules given here are only for the purpose of providing an overview of the general nature of real estate taxation. Do not rely on them; see a tax professional for tax advice.

TRAP

There are limitations to the types of deductions you can take on ordinary income. For example, tax and mortgage deductions can normally be taken only for your principal residence and one additional home. These deductions do not apply if you rent out your house. If you're a landlord, then you've got a business, and it's subject to all sorts of other taxation rules—see an accountant.

The True Value of Deducting Interest and Taxes

The true value of deducting your homeownership interest and taxes from your taxable ordinary income varies depending on your tax bracket. For example, let's say that your monthly mortgage *interest* is $2,000, and your *taxes* calculated monthly are another $400, for a total of $2,400. You should be able to take that $2,400 as a deduction from your taxable ordinary income each month.

Calculating Your Interest and Tax Deduction

Monthly mortgage interest	$2,000
Property taxes (calculated monthly)	400
Total deductions from taxable ordinary income	$2,400

No, you don't get to take the $2,400 a month in interest and property taxes off the amount you pay in income taxes. That would be a *tax credit*. Here we're talking a *tax deduction,* and it reduces your *taxable income*.

The actual cash value of a $2,400 deduction is determined by your tax bracket. The higher the tax bracket, the greater the value. The lower the tax bracket, the lesser the value.

If, for example, you're in the 28 percent bracket, the cash value is $672 a month. That's how much the deduction for mortgage interest and property taxes saves you in actual cash.

See Table 1.2 for the value of a $2,400 deduction in different tax brackets.

TRAP

Be careful not to confuse a *deduction* with a *tax credit*. Interest and taxes are *deductions*. They are deducted from your ordinary income, *not from your taxes*. (A tax credit is deducted from your taxes.) This means that the deduction is only worth as much as your marginal tax bracket.

Let's say that, as in our example, your tax deductions are valued at $672 a month. That's how much you'll save each month that you would otherwise pay Uncle Sam in taxes.

TABLE 1.2 Federal Tax Savings on a $2,400 Interest and Tax Deduction by Marginal Tax Bracket*

TAX BRACKET	TAX SAVINGS
10%	$240
15%	$360
25%	$600
28%	$672
33%	$792
35%	$840

*Check with your accountant to determine your tax bracket and actual savings.

Then, of course, there's the deduction you get from your state taxes. These vary widely, but if we assume you're in a 5 percent state tax bracket, then you would have an additional $120 in tax savings. (The amount will vary, of course, according to your state tax bracket, assuming you're in a state that collects income taxes and allows interest and property tax deductions.)

Now, let's go back. You buy instead of rent. And instead of paying $1,500 a month as a renter to a landlord, you're required to pay $2,500 a month to a mortgage lender, but the government kicks back $792 a month. So your out-of-pocket increase to move from being a renter to an owner is only $208 a month.

Difference between Renting and Owning

Monthly ownership payment*	$2,500
Less value of interest and tax deductions†	792
True monthly cost	1,708
Current rent	1,500
True cost to move up to ownership	$ 208

*Principal, interest, taxes, and insurance (PITI).
†Kicked back by government.

TIP

The higher the tax bracket, the more the benefit. In higher tax brackets, it could actually save you money to own instead of rent.

TRAP

There may be other costs of ownership we haven't counted such as homeowner's fees, if any. There are also going to be repair and maintenance costs that you don't have to pay as a tenant. (That's why it pays to buy a newer home than an older one: there's usually little to no repair and maintenance on newer properties.)

The Ownership Advantage

Given the advantages of ownership (leverage, inflation, and equity return), isn't it worth a hundred dollars or so a month increase to move from renting to owning?

It's important to keep our eyes on the donut and not the hole. Because of the value of deductions allowed for mortgage interest and taxes, the monthly payment for ownership is much less than most people imagine.

Further, keep in mind that I've chosen an extreme example—going from $1,500 a month rent to $2,500 a month ownership. The difference might be far less. Indeed, in many cases you can actually *save money each month* by converting from a renter to an owner!

The point, however, is that Uncle Sam is there to help you out, to encourage you to make a home purchase.

And remember, all this is *before* calculating profits that can be attributed to leverage, inflation, and equity return.

TIP

Take the deduction monthly. In other words, as soon as you own property, you can have your take-home pay adjusted upward to reflect that fact. Consult with your accountant, and have a new W-4 form sent to your employer that reflects your new deductions. That way instead of waiting until tax time in April, you can get the increased benefits of interest and property tax deductions paid to you monthly in the form of increased take-home pay. That definitely will help you make the payments.

Owning versus Renting: The Comparison

Okay, now let's be sure we're clear on this. You're a renter, and when you pay your rent each month to your landlord, *none* of the following happens:

- The government doesn't give you a deduction for the interest on the property you're renting. (That goes to the owner.)
- The government doesn't give you a deduction for the taxes on the property you're renting. (That also goes to the owner.)
- You get no benefit from price inflation. (Again, the owner gets that.)
- You get no benefit from leveraging the purchase. (Any wise owner is taking advantage of this.)
- You get no equity return. (That darned owner wins here again!)

After seeing all of this, why do you still want to rent instead of buy a home?

The Other Benefits

Let's not forget that there are some other intangible yet very important benefits to homeownership. These include the following:

- **More security.** When you rent, you're really at the mercy of the landlord when it comes to security. How do you know that the person the landlord rented to in the apartment next door isn't a criminal? Or doesn't have criminal intents?

  When you own, the person next door is also normally an owner. Of course, he or she also could be a criminal. But crime statistics show that most crimes almost universally are higher in transient areas such as rental properties than in areas where there are individual property owners. Further, owners tend to look out for each other's property.

  Besides, if you're concerned, as an owner you can take steps to make your property more secure including hardening windows and doors, putting in deadbolts, and installing electronic security systems.
- **Lower-density living.** Those who rent apartments generally have the highest-density living. Those who own

single-family detached homes usually have the lowest density.
Even condos are typically less dense than rental apartments.

Which do you prefer: the noise and congestion of high-density living? Or the relaxed atmosphere of low-density lifestyles?

- **Retirement nest eggs.** Finally, there's the matter of saving for retirement. Nearly everyone is concerned about this, and most people do put away something, but very few save enough. Except for their home. For many people this is their ace in the hole.

    After living in an owned home for much of their lives, many people sell that property and use the cash as a nest egg. Then they downsize to a smaller property, often in a lower-cost-of-living area, and the result is that they have more money to live on than they would have had otherwise.

    Without homeownership, millions of people in this country simply could not afford to retire to a lifestyle they could enjoy.

Ownership Drawbacks

It's often pointed out that two of the biggest drawbacks of home-ownership are repairs and maintenance. You're always painting the house, putting in new carpeting and flooring, landscaping, replacing heaters, and on and on. Who needs that bother?!

True enough. All of these items can be bothersome. However, most owners have been willing to bear them, given the enormous profits reaped over the last few years.

And if repairs and maintenance are too problematic for you, well, then you can always purchase a condo. You pay a monthly fee, and someone else takes care of most of the external repairs and maintenance for you. (You don't even have to wait for the roofer or the painter to show up because there's typically a management service that will do that for you.)

Condo owners do, however, have to be responsible for repairs and maintenance to the *interior* of their units (and in some cases, some of the exterior as well). But, then again, most renters have some responsibilities for breakage and other damage they cause.

The Name of the Game

It's often been said that America is a land of immigrants.

And what is the first thing that most immigrants do after arriving and, perhaps, setting up a family business? (Many, if not most, new small family businesses are run by immigrants.) They buy a home.

Immigrants know a lesson that many Americans born in this country have yet to learn—homeownership leads to prosperity. Historically it's always been the land owners in Asia and South and Central America and Europe who were prosperous and the renters who were impoverished. The trouble, of course, is that in most other countries, it's more difficult (in some countries nearly impossible) for most people to buy their own home. The relationship between incomes and prices make it prohibitive. And even where there is a good income, there's little or only very expensive financing.

Here in America, however, it's not only possible for nearly everyone to buy a home but it's also easy. As we've seen with deductions, the government even encourages it!

Furthermore, you can own more than one home. You too can become a landlord and have others make your monthly payments for you.

But the Market's Uncertain

It's easy to feel at ease about buying property when the market's going up. When that's the case, there are constant stories in the media about how prices are up this month over last, this year over last year, and so on. When you buy, you can feel comfortable that your home will be worth more tomorrow than what you paid for it today. (Of course, chances are you'll have to pay a record high price for that home in a *hot* market.)

But what about when prices are steady or, as they describe it in the industry, "moving sideways"? What about when there's little to no price appreciation?

Or, even worse, what about when prices are actually declining?

Although the real estate market often slows down and moves sideways, it rarely declines. Yet declining prices can happen during a real estate recession as occurred during the mid-1990s. It will surely happen again.

Sideways and declining markets bring with them great bargain opportunities. Many of those who got in over their head with creative financing when the market was booming, now must sell quickly to get out from under high payments. They will offer deep discounts for a quick sale.

Those who can't sell and can't make their new higher payments will lose their homes to foreclosure, and the lenders will now offer them for resale as "real estate owned" (REO) by lenders, also at deep discounts.

If you're looking to get into a home, a sideways or declining market is actually the *best* time to buy. You can get in at a bargain price and then take advantage of price increases once the market turns around and heads up again.

TIP Since the Great Depression of the 1930s, the real estate market in this country has moved in roughly 14-year cycles. There are about 7 up years and then 7 sideways or declining years. Seldom have the peaks and valleys been so steep, however, as the down years of the 1990s and the up years of the early 2000s.

Historically the real estate market in this country has always rebounded. If you need proof of this, consider the following: If someone were to offer you a property at 1910 prices, would you buy it?

You'd be crazy not to. Back in 1910 you could buy a lot in the heart of San Francisco, San Diego, Chicago, and even parts of New York City for under a thousand dollars.

What about 1940 prices? The same lot by then would have quadrupled in value, yet still cost only a few thousand dollars. Again, you'd be crazy not to leap at such an opportunity.

What about the 1950s and 1960s? By then, a building craze was putting houses on those lots. Back then you could buy a three-bedroom, two-bath house in the suburbs for the amazing price of $7,000. (That's the total price, not the down payment!)

Prices increased again in the 1970s and the 1980s. Then prices moved sideways or down in the 1990s, but by the year 2000, the median home price in the United States was $125,000. Would you buy a house at that price if given the opportunity today? (Today the median price is well over $200,000.)

The point is that while the price of real estate isn't a steady line upward, it has been a zigzag line upward. There are short-term ups and downs, but historically, the trend has always been up.

Thus when you buy today, even if you buy while the market is moving sideways, or even declining, all you have to do is hang on, and eventually a few years down the road, chances are excellent that you'll make a profit.

And remember, regardless of the market, you've got leverage, inflation, and equity return on your side.

TIP

You can't always time the market right—it's hard to be ready to buy just when it's the best time to buy. But you can almost always make a profit in real estate simply by hanging on long enough.

Does It Ever Pay to Rent Instead of Buy?

Yes, of course. In certain limited circumstances, renting makes more sense. Here are some of the circumstances in which it would be preferable to be a tenant.

When Renting Makes More Sense

- **When you're going to be in an area for a short time.** You may be on a short-term contract or in a short-term employment situation or going to school for a semester or two such that you are likely to be transferred in six months or a year. Unless the real estate market is superhot (meaning you can quickly flip a property), renting makes more sense. Remember, when you buy, usually there are high transfer costs—typically 10 percent of the cost of the purchase to buy and resell (including escrows, title searches, agent's commission, and so on). You should own the property long enough for inflation, equity return, and price appreciation to cover these costs.

- **When the differential between owning and renting is too high.** In one of our examples, it cost $1,500 to rent and $2,500 to buy. The monthly cost to buy was 40 percent higher than to rent. However, we saw that when the government offered deductions for mortgage interest and property taxes, things tended to even out—particularly for those in higher tax brackets.

    However, what if the differential is not $1,000 but instead $1,500 or $2,000 or $5,000 or more? What if it's not 40 percent but 60 percent? Or 100 percent? At some point the differential between renting and buying becomes so great that renting for a time (until the differential resets) makes more sense. (See the calculations below.)

- **When the market is in steep decline.** This rarely happens. But it would be a mistake to believe it can't or won't happen. At some point if properties are losing value, it may make more sense to rent temporarily. For example, it's hard to justify ownership if properties are losing value at 10 percent a year (admittedly, a rare occurrence that few of us have seen).

Calculating Whether It Makes More Sense to Own or to Rent

It is possible to rather scientifically determine whether renting or owning is a better deal for you. Making the calculation, of course, requires that you also make assumptions including how long you plan to live in the property, what the market will do during that time frame, your costs for financing as well as renting, and so on. Here's how it looks:

Assumptions You Need to Make

Time frame. How long will you own the property? The national average time a family owns a home is seven to nine years.

Rent increases. How much will your rent increase each year?

Financing costs. What is the interest rate on your mortgage?

Property taxes. Will they stay constant? These usually increase slightly on an annual basis.

Transaction costs. Closing costs are a big part of the deal. The average costs are usually 7 to 10 percent to buy and resell.

Annual appreciation. The historic average is around 5 percent, but it will vary.

Annual maintenance. How much will you have to pay? This amount varies depending on the home's condition and age.

Equity return. This sum is only available on amortized mortgages.

How to Calculate Your Cost to Rent a Home

FORMULA Months × rental rate × rental rate increase = rental costs

EXAMPLE 96 months (8 years) × $1,500 (rental rate) × 3 percent a year average rate increase = $162,000

Note: We're not counting utilities, which you'll normally pay whether you own or rent, or renter's insurance, which you probably will want.

How to Calculate Your Cost to Buy a Home

FORMULA Monthly payment [Months × (monthly payment − tax advantages) + maintenance] + transactions costs − appreciation − equity return = ownership costs

EXAMPLE   [96 months (8 years) × $1,708* + $100 monthly = $163,968] + $18,000 (transaction costs) − $87,360† (appreciation) − $18,000‡ (equity return) = $76,608

---

*Monthly payment including mortgage insurance is $2,500 minus $792 for taxes and interest (see calculation above) equals $1,708.

†$200,000 at 5 percent a year over 8 years = $87,360.

‡Equity return: Assume a 100 percent loan-to-value (LTV) mortgage of $200,000 fully amortized (pays itself off) over 30 years. The equity return over 96 months (the first 8 years) roughly equals $18,000. (To get the actual equity return, consult one of the online wizards such as those found at www.eloan.com.)

Comparison Between Rental Costs and Ownership Costs

Rental costs	$162,000
Ownership costs	76,608
Difference	$ 85,392

In our example it costs over $85,000 more over eight years to rent than to own.

Further, at the end of those eight years if you rent, you've got nothing to show for it. At the end of eight years of ownership, you've got that $85,392 in equity in your house that you can cash out.

Note that the formulas can be used in what-if situations. For example, *what if* the annual rate of appreciation is zero over eight years? Or *what if* rent increases average 10 percent a year? The result you'll get from these formulas will vary, sometimes dramatically depending on the assumptions you make. No assurance is given that the assumptions made for the examples above will be accurate over time.

What If You Still Can't Afford It?

If after this discussion you still don't want to own your own home, I'd be very surprised. But, then again, maybe you can't afford to buy.

If that were the case, I'd be even more surprised. In the next chapters we're going to look at how you can use your rent money to buy your own home. We're going to see how almost anyone in this country can do this. And that, my friend, includes you.

Do Market Conditions Really Count?

There's an old adage, attributed to George Santayana, that goes, "Those who cannot remember the past are condemned to repeat it." Certainly there's truth there. However, my own version is, "Those who don't recall the past can't take advantage of the present."

Whatever real estate market conditions are at the moment, everywhere I look there are people—would-be home buyers and investors—who are making the assumption that this is the way it's always been and this is the way it always will be. Sad to say, too many of us suffer from a lack of historical perspective.

For example, when you read this, the real estate market may be down or moving sideways or even be zooming up. It's only natural, if you're new to the field, to assume the way you now see it is the way it is, always. But that simply isn't so. When you take the perspective of a couple of years, or only one year, you tend to get a skewered picture. It's only when you look long term—decades—that a clearer picture emerges.

I once heard a lecturer talk about oak trees. The mighty oak tree can live for hundreds of years. But, this lecturer said, imagine a visitor from outer space who happens to visit our planet and is here for only one day. He lands near an oak tree and admires its height and the strength of its wood. He then notices a few acorns lying on the ground. Picking them up, he wonders what sort of a species they are, and then he discards them. Because his observations cover only a single day, he never makes the connection between the humble acorn and the mighty oak. For him to see the relationship, he would have to watch the development of the acorn for decades to see how it would grow into an oak tree.

The real estate market is like that. When it was booming in one of its great expansions roughly between 1999 and 2006, a person who saw it only then would, naturally enough, assume that real estate values always grow 10 to 25 percent a year. Many, too many, people made that assumption and bought one, two, or a dozen homes hoping to multiply their profits.

When the so-called bubble burst in 2006, lots of these people found themselves strapped with properties they couldn't afford. They tried to cut their selling prices to dump them. Many lost them to foreclosure. Those on the sidelines who would normally buy got scared and stayed out of the market. And when the inventory of unsold houses skyrocketed, prices fell dramatically.

To gain a wider perspective, let's take a different but also recent example, one that too few people remember. There was a deep real estate recession roughly between 1991 and 1998 in most areas of the country. The inventory of unsold homes was huge. Prices not only didn't move up, in many areas they moved down. Declines of as much as 25 to 30 percent were common in some markets. People couldn't sell their property "for love or money." Auctions of homes by lenders who had taken them back in foreclosure were common.

During that time, people who thought about coming into the market and saw only the hard times made the erroneous assumption that real estate would always be down. Hence, many stayed away. They frequently rented instead of buying. They saw those who had earlier paid too much for their properties now suffering, and they didn't want any part of it.

However, their perspective was as jaded in the long term as those who saw only the boom market after the turn of the century. One saw only boom. One saw only bust. And neither made the connection.

Like that alien who was here for only a single day and never made the association between the acorn and the oak, these investors never made the connection between the down market of the 1990s and the up market of the early 2000s. They saw them as independent of each other.

In contrast, a very few people realized what was happening, and they bought for the long term during the 1990s when the market was down, and later on they sold for huge profits during the 2000s when the market was up. (And if the market is down when you read this, they are buying again.)

The moral of this story is to keep your eye on the long term—not just on a single year or two. Don't be like that alien who sees only a single day in a hundred-year life cycle. Don't see real estate as it is today and think that's the way it will be tomorrow.

Try to learn from the past.

Tomorrow's Market

What will real estate be like a year from now? Three years? Five years? Ten years?

If you knew that, you could position yourself to take advantage of coming changes. You could play the market for big profits.

I don't have a crystal ball that can predict the future . . . and neither does anyone else. However, if we count on the future to be somewhat like the past, we can get some idea of how it should play out over the next decade.

Real Estate Facts You Should Know

- Over the past 50 years, the *average* rate of annual price appreciation for residential property has been about *5 percent* a year.
- Since the Great Depression of the 1930s, real estate has moved in cycles lasting approximately *14 years*—7 years of expansion followed by 7 years of weakening followed by a new expansion of 7 years and so on and on.
- As Will Rogers, the famous American raconteur, was fond of saying about real estate, "Better buy some now because they ain't making any more of it!"

If the market happens to be moving *sideways* (meaning not much price appreciation, not much weakening—a balance between buyers and sellers) *or* if it happens to be actually declining, does this mean it's a bad time to move from renting to owning?

In the short term, perhaps. Since it's almost impossible to peg the exact bottom of the market, you could conceivably buy while prices are declining and find that your home is worth a bit less next year than you paid for it. No one likes to be in that situation.

But what about the long term? What about into the next decade? If we look at the past, we can see that the chances are excellent that a new real estate boom is just beyond the horizon. That just as the prices of the 1990s seemed ridiculously low judged by the prices of the early 2000s, the prices of today might seem just as ridiculously low judged by the prices of tomorrow.

Don't be shortsighted. Don't be one of those naysayers who say things like, "Stay away from real estate—it's a bad investment." Seldom are investments bad or good, per se. Sometimes it's just a matter of timing. Buy while the price is down and ride the wave to higher profits, and any investment will seem great.

Can You Get Hurt?

Thirty-five years ago, my brothers and I were buying all the real estate we could get our hands on in northern California. The market was moving sideways—if we saw a 2 to 3 percent price appreciation in a year, we were happy. We didn't care—we were buying for the long term.

I remember my older brother telling me, "The only investment you can't get hurt on is real estate!"

Well, with all due respect to my older brother, that's not necessarily so. If you buy with the wrong terms and have payments you can't afford, then you could get hurt by losing your property to foreclosure. If you buy intending to flip in a few months and the market turns on you, you could get burned badly. The neighborhood could turn. And there are other ways you could get hurt too.

But the essence of what he said contains an element of truth. If you buy wisely for the long term and hang onto your properties, they will come through for you. If you buy a home, move into it, and live there, over the years it should make your financial dreams a reality.

How Can House Prices Go Higher?

There used to be a popular radio show host in Los Angeles called Hilly Rose, and when I wrote my first book, *How to Buy and Sell Real Estate for Financial Security* (McGraw-Hill), back in 1978, he invited me to be on his show. I distinctly remember him asking me, "How can the market possibly go higher? I own a $125,000 home in one of the best areas of Los Angeles, and you're telling me that it's going to be worth even more in price. I find it difficult to believe."

A $125,000 home in one of the best areas of Los Angeles? Today, you'd be lucky to find a shack in such an area for under $5 million.

Never get overimpressed with housing prices. We always get to the point where we seem to have topped out the market. And yet, in a year or so, the prices seem to go even higher.

There is no ceiling on the price of real estate. As long as demand remains strong and the supply limited (remember Will Rogers' quote), the price has only one direction to go in the long run—up.

TRAP

Don't try to time the real estate market perfectly. If there's one thing I've learned, it's that it's only possible to pick the high point and the low point, afterward. Hindsight is great, but foresight leaves a lot to be desired. Get in at almost any point, and hang on for the long term. History suggests sooner rather than later you'll be a winner.

Where Is the Market Now?

I'm sure that after our discussion thus far, there are many readers who feel it would be helpful to know just where the real estate market is currently. It's certainly something to factor into a decision on whether to buy or rent.

The Local Real Estate Market

To answer that question, it's first important to understand that the real estate market, like politics, is all local. While it may be booming in Los Angeles, it might be collapsing in south Florida. Expansion in Seattle, retreat in Boston.

Thus when you hear on the national news on television or the radio or even the Internet that the "real estate market" is soaring or plummeting, take it with a grain of salt. From a practical standpoint, what really matters is only what's happening in your neck of the woods, in your city and neighborhood. If your real estate market is expanding because of new jobs coming into the area and prices are escalating because of a housing shortage, you're in the middle of a boom. This is true even if most of the rest of the country is in a bust.

TRAP

Be particularly careful about the source of news that you get. Some media have a vested interest in other investment venues such as stocks and bonds, bullion, rarities, or whatever. Consider the motivation and source when someone blasts or praises real estate, including this writer.

The Local Unsold Inventory

Next, pay attention to the *unsold inventory* of homes in your area. Around 90 percent of homes for sale are listed with agents, and the vast majority of these agents belong to a multiple listing service (MLS) operated by their state real estate board. One of the functions of an MLS system is to track the number of listed and unsold homes. This information is sometimes expressed as the number of days it takes the average listed home to sell. Of course, it stands to reason that the higher the inventory, the longer it takes to sell.

What you need to watch is the trend. Is the inventory increasing? Is the time it takes to sell getting longer?

If six months ago it took only a month to sell an average home and now it takes four months, that tells you the market is softening. But if the figures go the other way, it tells you the market is getting tighter.

If inventories are increasing quickly, it suggests that prices will soon level off, if not fall, because the supply of homes is going up.

Basic economics suggests that an increasing supply without a corresponding increase in demand will eventually lead to lower prices as people anxious to sell cut what they're willing to take for their home.

Of course, if inventories are decreasing, the opposite is true: tightening supplies in the face of strong demand suggest eventual increases in prices.

You should be able get these kinds of statistics from any real estate agent. Nearly all offices today are computerized, and almost any agent should be able to pop up the figures with a few clicks on a keyboard. Most agents are happy to provide you with this information on a complimentary basis in the hope that if and when you decide to buy, you'll use their services.

Be Wary of Headlines

Newspapers in particular seem to love to scare their readers. I can recall seeing headlines announcing that the last real estate "bubble" was "bursting" as early as 2003. That was probably three years before the market took a dip and certainly before the biggest price increases occurred. Similarly, just as the market was turning, I saw headlines announcing, "Biggest gains in history."

TIP

Fear and greed seem to sell papers. So taking the time to learn the facts is what makes for good investments in any field.

But Can I Afford It?

There are about 35 million rental homes in this country (U.S. Census Bureau) occupied by approximately 100 million renters. Are you one of those renters?

Why?

After reading the last two chapters and seeing the profits and advantages of homeownership during boom times and recessions, I can't believe you'd like to keep on renting.

But, you may say, you can't afford to own. You don't have money saved. You don't have a big enough income. You don't know how or where to start.

In this chapter we're going to refute some fallacies about traditional home buying. Then in the next two chapters we'll look at creative tools, such as lease options and contracts of sale, that make it even easier to buy.

Fallacies to Be Disproved

1. I don't have the down payment.
2. I don't have the closing costs.
3. My credit is too bad.
4. I can't afford the payments

Fallacy 1: I Can't Buy because I Don't Have the Down Payment

Are you sure you don't have it?

There are two elements at play here. The first is knowing how much of a down payment you really need. The second is knowing how much you actually have. (You may have more than you think!)

First, how much do you need?

Perhaps you have heard that the down payment required in real estate investing is 20 percent of the purchase price and that a lender will write a maximum loan of 80 percent. Up until the last few decades, that information was correct, and the 20 percent figure for down payments was carved in stone. So if the value of a house was $200,000, then a buyer would need 20 percent, or $40,000, to put down, which was a lot of cash back then and still is today.

Then, some savings and loans began offering what were considered to be amazing 90 percent loan-to-value (LTV) mortgages for their best customers. These mortgages required only 10 percent down. On a $200,000 home, that meant that the down payment required was halved to $20,000. (The *loan-to-value ratio* is the amount of the loan divided by the sales price of the property. This is a good term for you to be familiar with because it comes up a lot in mortgage discussions.)

Lenders began to be able to offer mortgages at higher than 80 percent LTVs because of the advent of private mortgage insurance (PMI), which covered the added risk. This insurance protected the lenders against loss. Today PMI is widely available, and it costs the borrower (who pays for it) about 1/4 to 1/2 percent *added* to the interest rate.

The 90 percent LTV mortgage stayed in place even after most savings and loans either collapsed or were gobbled up by other financial institutions in the 1980s.

Then, about 10 years ago, suddenly all the rules were relaxed. *Financial profiling* came into vogue. To lenders, this meant that based on your financial profile (which was, and still is, determined by a combination of your credit report, your credit score, and other factors such as your income and assets), they felt they could determine how good a credit risk you were. So rather than assuming your credit risk was dependent on how much money you put down, lenders now felt they could judge whether you were the type of person to keep making those payments. Financial profiling thus enabled them to identify a large class of buyer-borrowers who felt an obligation to avoid foreclosure regardless of the size of their down payment.

We're talking here about *financial* profiling. The lender looks at just your financial history. While any kind of racial, ethnic, familial, or other personal profiling is forbidden in this country, financial profiling is allowed.

Historically, the entire purpose of insisting on a large down payment was to assure lenders that you'd make the mortgage payments. The theory was that the more of your own money you had in the property, the more likely you were to avoid losing it to foreclosure no matter how dire your financial picture became. This assumption has actually been proven to be largely a fallacious concept. When times get rough, some people will bail out and others will stick it out, regardless of the down payment they originally made.

Voilá! Today, lenders using PMI and financial profiling are happy to make 95 percent LTV mortgages and even 100 percent LTV mortgages. As a buyer-borrower, if you fit the right profile, you are no longer required to put down 20 percent, or 10 percent, or even 5 percent. In fact, you can easily get an LTV mortgage of 100 percent.

The key, of course, is having the right profile. This generally means an unblemished credit report, sufficient assets and income, and a credit score (FICO score) of around 700 or higher. According to lenders, more than half the people in the country qualify.

Note: The abbreviation FICO refers to the Fair Isaac Corporation. It's the leading credit rating organization in the country. It looks at your credit report and some other factors, and using computerized models, it rates you with a numeric score between 350 and 850. The higher the score, the better credit risk you are; the lower the score, the worse credit risk you are. We'll discuss credit ratings in more depth in Chapter 7, "Getting Financing Even When Credit Is a Problem."

TIP

Mortgages over 80 percent still require that you pay PMI, which adds to your monthly payment. You may be able to avoid paying the extra cost of PMI by getting two mortgages: a first for 80 percent and a second for up to 20 percent. Since the first is not higher than 80 percent, the lender doesn't require PMI. There is no PMI usually required on second mortgages. Also, as your property appreciates and your LTV ratio comes down, once it reaches about 79 percent, you may be able to have the PMI payment removed. Check with a good mortgage broker.

Do You Qualify for a No-Down-Payment Mortgage?

It's very easy to find out. Contact a mortgage broker and ask to be *preapproved* for a mortgage.

The broker will take an application from you (either in person, on the phone, or over the Internet) that requires you to answer about 60 questions. With the information you provide, the broker will then get your credit report and score, and he or she will also perhaps ask you for some documentation such as a salary payment stub or a bank statement. Within a few days, or in some cases just an hour or so, you'll know if you've been preapproved.

Mortgage brokers are in every community in the country, and they are listed as such both on the Internet and in the phone book. If you have a friend who recently had a good experience with a particular mortgage broker, you should consider his or her recommendation when you finally choose a mortgage broker to work with. Also, real estate agents, escrow officers, and others in the field of realty can usually recommend a mortgage broker.

Getting preapproved is usually free, although there may be a nominal $35 fee for the credit report, which usually is refunded if you eventually get a mortgage through the broker who obtained the report for you. Beware of any mortgage broker who wants to charge you a large fee for getting preapproved. You're getting snookered—look elsewhere.

If you qualify for a no-down-payment (100 percent LTV) mortgage, then you're on your way toward buying your own home without cash down. It's just that easy. On the other hand, perhaps your credit profile indicates that you're not likely to get a 100 percent LTV loan. Maybe you'll be asked to come up with 5 or 10 percent down. (Today, very few lenders ask for more than 10 percent down, *although they will ask for higher down payments from borrowers with credit challenges,* which we'll discuss later in this chapter.)

Let's assume that in your case you can't get a no-down-payment mortgage but instead need to come up with 10 percent down. What are you going to do now?

Options When You Can't Get a No-Down-Payment Mortgage

In real estate there are almost always alternatives. If you find that you need to put cash down, here are some of the many ways available to come up with the money.

Alternatives When You Need a Down Payment

1. **Come up with the cash.** Many people do have the money squirreled away in savings accounts, stock or bond accounts, and elsewhere. (Beware of using retirement money to buy a home—check with your accountant first.) Also, you may be able to borrow from relatives.

2. **Get the seller to put up the down payment.** Depending on how motivated the seller is, he or she may give you a second mortgage or even a straight note for all of the down payment money. Just be sure that your lender allows this; see the explanation later in this chapter.

3. **Use a lease option or a contract for sale.** This would mean using your rent money directly to come up with the down payment: you literally "rent to own." We'll look into these methods in depth in Chapters 4 and 5.

There are other means as well, and we'll discuss them later in this book. What's important to come away from this discussion with is the knowledge that you can get into a home with a nothing-down mortgage or find the cash for a down payment.

The truth is that today, virtually no one should be stopped from making a purchase of a home because they don't have a down payment.

TRAP

Beware if you're offered a "subprime" nothing-down mortgage. It is sometimes offered to buyers who don't qualify for a prime mortgage as described above. It often carries a much higher interest rate, increased closing costs, and may reset after a few years to a much higher payment. As of this writing, a significant number of borrowers in foreclosure are those who got nothing-down subprime mortgages. See below for details.

Fallacy 2: I Can't Buy because I Don't Have the Closing Costs

Most people buying real estate *under*estimate their closing costs. For a buyer, closing costs can sometimes be as much as 5 percent or more of the purchase price. For example, if you're purchasing a $300,000 home, you might have as much as $15,000 in closing costs.

Yes, they probably will be lower. But my feeling is that it's always best to estimate on the high side. That way, if you're wrong, you're not going to get hurt.

But, you say, if you don't have the money for the down payment, where are you going to get the money for the closing costs? The 5 percent figure comes to $15,000 cash on a $300,000 purchase. Were you asked to put, for example, 10 percent down and then add in another 5 percent for closing costs, that's a total of 15 percent? On a $300,000 purchase, that's $45,000. Either way, you say, you certainly don't have that much money.

In the previous section, we saw how to eliminate the down payment. Here, we're going to look at how to eliminate, or at least shift, the closing costs to someone else. First, let's see which closing costs you will have to pay. Then we'll see what to do about them.

TRAP

Closing costs must be paid. Either they're paid by you, or they're paid by someone else.

What Are the Closing Costs?

The actual distribution of closing costs will vary for each transaction. However, here are some typical closing costs. The amounts have been purposely estimated a bit high.

Estimate of Buyer's Closing Costs on a $300,000 Purchase

- **Mortgage points.** These are fees demanded by the lender usually to increase the yield of the loan. The lower the interest rate, generally speaking, the more the points. The higher the interest rate, the fewer the points. Each point is 1 percent of the mortgage.

If we assume a 100 percent LTV (no-down-payment mortgage) and 3 points, the amount is $9,000.

- **Mortgage fees.** These are additional fees charged by the lender.

  In our example, assume $1,000.

- **Title insurance.** This sum guarantees that you will have clear title. Sometimes the buyer and seller split it.

  We'll assume you have to pay: $1,500.

- **Escrow cost.** Typically buyers and sellers split escrow costs, which are charges involved with setting up escrow accounts. The charges vary greatly.

  We'll assume 1/2 percent of the purchase price to you, or $1,500.

- **Home inspection.** You pay this fee to an inspector to tell you if there are any undisclosed defects in the property.

  We'll assume for our example this fee is $350.

- **Miscellaneous costs.** These could be anything from an agent's administrative fee to a charge for an attorney's services.

  We'll say for our example that these fees will be $1,000.

So for your purchase of a $300,000 property, the closing costs could come to roughly $14,350, or almost 5 percent of the purchase price. You can either dig deep into your pocket and pay them. Or . . . ?

Solution 1: Have the Lender Pay Your Closing Costs

Today *no-closing-cost mortgages* are quite common. There are no costs to be paid by you out of pocket. Rather, all the costs are handled by the lender.

Of course, the terminology is rather deceptive. There *are* closing costs. It's just that they are wrapped up in the mortgage so that you don't see them. There are two methods commonly used to accomplish this.

Method 1: Increase the Loan Amount to Cover the Closing Costs. In other words, the amount of your loan in our example would be increased by $14,350 to $314,350. And then the lender would take the additional money from the mortgage and use it to pay all of your closing costs. Of course, the slightly bigger loan would result in a slightly higher monthly payment for you (about $80 monthly at a 7 percent interest rate) and a considerable amount of increased interest over the term of the loan.

TRAP

Sometimes lenders who offer nothing-down financing (100 percent LTV) will refuse to increase the loan amount to cover the costs of the closing. They reckon that they are already at 100 percent, so they won't go higher. (They are usually allowed by the government to go up to 125 percent of the LTV.) Further, financial profiling has sometimes suggested that those who can't come up with their closing costs may be at greater risk of later defaulting on their loan.

Method 2: Increase the Interest Rate to Cover the Closing Costs. Here *the amount you borrow remains the same.* However, the interest rate you pay goes up, typically by $1/4$ to $3/8$ of 1 percent. For example, if you were quoted an interest rate of 7 percent, by wrapping the closing costs into the mortgage, the rate might go up to $7\frac{1}{4}$ or $7\frac{3}{8}$ percent.

That also would mean a slight increase in monthly payments. On a $300,000 mortgage at a fixed rate for 30 years, the difference in payments between 7 and $7\frac{3}{8}$ percent is about $80 monthly. Wrapping the closing costs into the mortgage would cost you that much more a month. Of course, that's roughly $14,000, in our example, that you wouldn't have to take out of your pocket.

The return to the lender is increased by the higher interest rate. The lender, in turn, uses that increased money to pay your closing costs.

Some lenders who will hesitate to increase the loan amount to cover the closing costs will be positively happy to increase the interest rate to cover them.

TIP

Lenders may be unwilling to wrap *all* of your closing costs into the mortgage. They may sometimes balk at such items as a real estate agent's administrative fees, an inspection report fee, or an attorney's fees. In that case, you'd have to come up with these yourself or use a different option (such as having the seller pay the costs) as described below.

How Do I Get a Lender to Wrap My Closing Costs into the Mortgage? Be sure to tell your mortgage broker that you want the loan to cover your closing costs. That way the mortgage broker can steer you to a lender who handles things in this manner on a regular basis. (You can even specify this condition when you ask a mortgage broker to arrange for preapproval for you, but if you switch mortgage brokers later, remember to restate this condition.)

If the lender you are given refuses to cover closing costs, or if your mortgage broker can't find a lender who does, look elsewhere. There are thousands of mortgage brokers nationwide, and most can work anywhere within the state in which they are licensed. (Some states, such as California, do not specifically license mortgage brokers but only require them to have a general real estate license.) And there are also thousands of lenders. You have choices here. Lots of them.

Remember, you shouldn't go to a lender hat in hand. You're there to make the lender money. As such, you should be treated not only with respect but also as a privileged client who gets the best service and the best mortgages and rates. Don't get what you want and need? Use your feet to find a more receptive lender.

Solution 2: Have the Seller Pay Your Closing Costs

Just as we noted above that sellers may be willing to cover your down payment, they may also be willing to cover your closing costs. In fact, it's usually far easier to get a seller to cover closing costs than it is to get a seller to cover a down payment.

Whenever the markets are a bit slow, sellers are looking for ways to incentivize buyers. That can mean offering to pay closing costs.

TRAP

Lenders may not give you a mortgage if the seller pays *all* of your closing costs. However, they are very likely to be amenable if the seller pays your *nonrecurring closing costs*. These are costs such as title insurance, escrow fees, and some loan fees that occur only once, at the time of the transaction. (*Recurring closing costs* would refer to such expenses as taxes, insurance, and mortgage interest.)

How Do I Get a Seller to Pay My Closing Costs? Make it a condition of sale. Have your agent insert a clause into the purchase offer saying that the sale is *contingent* on the sellers paying your nonrecurring closing costs. Either they pay them, or you don't buy the property. (See also Chapter 6.)

Many times, especially in slow markets, the sellers will go along. Of course, keep in mind that if the sellers aren't agreeable, you won't have a purchase!

Fallacy 3: I Can't Buy because My Credit Is Bad

You've got no money for a down payment, no money for closing costs, *and* you've got bad credit. I suppose you're expecting me to say, "Tough luck—you can't buy!"

Fortunately, that's not the case. There are at least two ways that you can still purchase a home even in your situation. (Of course, it's a lot easier if you have some cash to cover the down payment and closing costs. But, even if you don't, it's not impossible to own your home.)

Method 1: Look for a Subprime Loan and Lender

Prime refers to those who have top credit and can get the best loans such as those described earlier. *Subprime* means everybody else. You can probably be a subprime candidate in the following circumstances.

Reasons You May Be a Subprime Borrower

- You have some blemishes on your credit report.
- You have a credit score lower than 680 (FICO).
- You have had a recent foreclosure or bankruptcy. (Although either of these within the previous two years may mean an institutional lender will not grant you any kind of mortgage, you may still be able to own your home by getting a mortgage from the seller, as described in method 2 below.)

There are a limited number of subprime lenders, but a good mortgage broker will quickly be able to put you in touch with one. There is, however, a penalty to pay. Generally speaking, you will be charged a higher-than-market interest rate, sometimes much higher. This will mean higher monthly payments.

Also, you may be required to put additional money down to get a subprime mortgage. Instead of a 100 percent LTV mortgage, you could be required to come up with 5, 10, 20 percent, or more of the purchase price, depending on how bad your credit really is. (Beware of 100 percent subprime mortgages—see earlier TRAP.)

Method 2: Look for a Seller to Give You a Mortgage

Banks, savings and loans, and other lending institutions are not the only ones who give mortgages. Sellers give them too. No cash changes hands here.

In a *seller's mortgage*, the seller gives you a loan in the form of credit toward the purchase price. On a $250,000 purchase, the seller could credit you with as much as $250,000. That would be the equivalent of a 100 percent LTV loan. In this case, you'd make monthly mortgage payments to the seller instead of a bank. This is described as "the seller carrying back paper." In effect, the seller has become your lender.

Why would a seller give you a mortgage?

Typical Reasons Sellers Give Buyers Mortgages

- **To make the sale.** When the market isn't strong, sellers have difficulty moving their properties. One way to get out from under a home a seller's having difficulty selling is to help the buyer with the financing. That way a buyer who likes the property but can't get an institutional (bank) mortgage can make the purchase.

- **To earn more interest.** When sellers take cash from a house and then put it into a certificate of deposit (CD), probably the safest way to keep money, the interest they would receive on that money would normally be several percentage points lower than the going rate for mortgages. By giving you a mortgage, the sellers can increase the yield on their money sometimes by as much as 3 or 4 percent.

- **To get a higher price.** Sometimes there's a trade-off. The seller will give you a mortgage *if* you pay more for the property. You might have to pay 5 percent or more over market to get seller financing. Of course, it might well be worth it to you to be able to buy a home.

Not all sellers are willing or able to offer financing on the sale of their home. Many sellers, for example, owe very nearly as much as their home is worth. Hence, they have no equity to turn into seller financing. *Only a seller who has a substantial equity can offer seller financing.*

TRAP

When a seller owes *more* than the property is worth (after costs of sale), that seller is said to be *upside down*. In a real estate recession when prices are falling, sellers who recently purchased are often in this situation, and they certainly can't offer financing to a buyer.

What you need to look for are sellers who own their property free and clear or who have only a very small mortgage on it. It is estimated that roughly one-third of all property owners in this country own their homes outright with no mortgages, so you have a large pool to fish in.

Instruct your real estate agent that you want or need seller financing. Your agent should be able to cherry pick the listings until he or she comes up with a list of properties where the seller can afford to carry back a mortgage. Then look at those.

TIP

Many times sellers will not advertise in their listings that they are willing to handle seller financing. Rather, they simply don't say anything about it. In those cases, when the seller has a large equity in the property, you can make them an offer which includes their carrying back paper. Will the seller accept? You never know until you try. (You probably should avoid those sellers who specifically state that they do not want to carry back paper.)

Before agreeing to give you a mortgage, sellers very frequently will want a credit report and a credit score, just like the big lenders. However, unlike banks and other institutional lenders who make loans based on cold computerized assessments, sellers often look at the buyer in a personal way. If the seller likes you, decides you're honest but just have hit a hard spot in life, he or she may give you the mortgage regardless of what your credit report or score says. I've seen it happen many times. You may be able to get just the financing you need by making a good impression!

Fallacy 4: I Can't Buy because My Income Is Too Low and I Can't Afford the Payments

We've already seen how deducting mortgage interest and property taxes can lower the effective mortgage payment. But perhaps you feel it's still too high.

The mortgage broker with whom you get preapproved will tell you how big a payment you can get, based on the lender's analysis. That may or may not jibe with what you feel comfortable with.

TIP

No matter what amount the mortgage broker and lender say you can afford as a monthly payment, ask yourself if you'll feel comfortable with it. If you sense it's too high for you, don't make the leap. Remember, you have to make that payment each month, and neither the lender nor the mortgage broker will contribute a dime to help you.

However, when the mortgage broker tells you that you *can't* afford the payment on the property you want to buy, or when your gut tells you the same thing regardless of what the mortgage broker says, it's time to look for alternatives. Here are six ways to cut your monthly payment.

Method 1: Look for a Lower-Interest-Rate Loan

One way to cut your mortgage payment is to find a loan with a lower interest rate. The lower the interest rate, the lower the monthly payment.

While it's true that the market rate for mortgage interest is a standard across the country on any given day, there are small variances among lenders. For example, one lender may have tied up some money several months ago when the rate was lower (or higher) and hence can offer you a better (or worse) deal than other lenders. In other words, shop around. You may be pleasantly surprised.

Just be sure that you compare apples with apples—that is, the same kinds of loans with each other such as fixed rate with fixed rate or ARMs (adjustable-rate mortgages) with ARMs. If you compare two different kinds of loans, you could get wildly different interest rates that really aren't comparable (see the Appendix).

Method 2: Look for an Adjustable-Rate Mortgage (ARM)

The type of loan that you get can affect the amount of the monthly payments. For example, an adjustable-rate mortgage (ARM) will almost always have a lower *initial* interest rate than a fixed-rate loan. This can help you get into a property.

For example, the interest rate on a fixed-rate, $300,000, 30-year mortgage may be 7 percent, which translates into payments of $2,000 a month. On the other hand, the *start* rate on an ARM may be just 5 percent, which translates into about $1,610 a month—a savings of almost $400 a month. That could be the difference between being able to make the purchase . . . and not.

There is a trap, however.

Keep in mind that over time the interest rate for ARMs adjusts (hence the name) and usually goes up. So after a few years, you could end up paying as much as you would for a fixed-rate loan, often more. An ARM typically gives you a break on monthly payments when you *first* get the loan, but *later on* catches up and can hit you hard with higher payments.

Thus, the critical information for a borrower when getting an ARM is knowing for how long the initial low interest rate will last. For example, you might get an ARM with an initial interest rate fixed for three years at 5 percent, while the market rate for a standard fixed-rate mortgage might be 7 percent.

What's important to watch here is that three-year period. In a sense, you're getting a three-year loan, and in exchange, the lender will lower your interest rate. However, *after* three years, your rate resets to the market rate. In some loans it goes *above* the market rate to catch up for all the interest lost while it was low during the initial three years! (Which is why you may want to refinance or sell after the start-rate period.)

Many people feel an ARM with a low start rate is a great trade-off. It allows them to get into a property they couldn't otherwise afford. And they figure that when the start period ends (in three years in our example), they'll refinance to a new ARM or sell.

TRAP

The piper must be paid. At the end of three years, the loan usually resets (automatically) to an *adjustable* interest rate, and it jumps up to the market rate or higher. Some borrowers who recently reached the three-year mark in their loans saw their interest rates nearly double—likewise for their payments. At the same time the market softened so they couldn't resell. And, if their job situation worsens, they might not be able to refinance. Remember, three years isn't a very long time.

Typically ARMs will offer a lower initial interest rate at the following intervals and the mortgage payment will be lower, accordingly.

ARM Initial Interest Rate Reduction as It Affects Interest Rate

10 years
7 years
5 years
3 years
2 years
1 year
6 months
1 month

Less	**←**	**Interest Rate**	**→**	**More**

The Interest Rate Reduction on an Arm Increases the Shorter the Term and Decreases the Longer the Term

The longer the initial interval (sometimes called the *teaser*), the less of an interest start-rate reduction you're likely to get. The shorter the initial interval, the greater an interest start-rate reduction. Remember, the initial interest rate reduction is always *short term*.

Most borrowers feel that the optimum balance between lowering the interest rate and time is five years. I personally feel it's seven. I like the extra couple of years as insurance against hard times. However, you'll usually get a lower start rate on a five-year initial interval term and certainly on a three-year initial interval term than you will get on a seven-year initial interval term.

It's up to you. Just remember that when that initial (teaser) time is up, your interest rate and monthly payment will go up. At that point, you'll either have to pay the higher rate and payments, refinance (if you're able at the time), or sell (if you're able). It's definitely a risk.

Method 3: Look for a Short-Term Balloon Loan

With an ARM you have what is basically a 30-year loan combined with an initial short-term fixed interest rate. For example, for the first 3, 5, 7, or whatever number of years of the mortgage (teaser), the interest rate is fixed (at lower than the market rate). For the remaining 27, 25, or 23 years of the loan, the rate is adjustable and fluctuates at market rates. As we've seen, with this type of mortgage, once the rate switches to an adjustable term, the interest rate and payments typically skyrocket.

An alternative is the *balloon loan*. Here typically the rate is fixed for the entire loan period. While the mortgage is paid back (amortized) as if it were for 30 years, the term is much shorter, say, 5 or 7 years. At the end of the term, the entire remaining balance comes due—that is, it "balloons."

Balloon loans are just like the adjustable-rate mortgages we were speaking of earlier. Except that at the end of the start period for a balloon loan, the whole remaining balance is due, while with an ARM, the loan then switches to adjustable-rate terms.

The advantage of a balloon mortgage is that some lenders will give you a terrific reduction in interest rate (and monthly payment) for this type of loan. After all, they know that within a short time, you'll have to pay back the money. (If you don't pay it back, they'll take the property through foreclosure and resell it, something many lenders have become quite adroit at doing.)

The danger to you is that when the balloon comes due, it's due. Your usual choices are to pay off the mortgage by either refinancing the house or selling it. The great danger, of course, is that because of your personal finances at the time or market conditions, you might not be able to do either.

Method 4: Look for an Interest-Only Loan

The name says it all.

Here the mortgage does not *amortize*—that is, it does not pay itself off over time. Instead of paying monthly both principal and interest, you pay only interest. Thus, at the end of the term, whether it is 3 years or 30, you owe as much as you originally borrowed. (You might actually owe more, depending on the type of loan—see negatively amortized mortgages below.)

The advantage of an interest-only mortgage is that you have a lower monthly payment than you would have with a mortgage that pays itself off. Let's take an example.

You borrow $200,000 at 6 percent for 30 years. On a fully amortized (pays itself off) mortgage, your monthly payments are $1,200 a month.

However, on the same $200,000 at the same interest rate for the same term, but *at interest only*, your payments drop to $1,000 a month—a savings of $200 monthly. By paying just the interest and not the principal, you've got a monthly mortgage reduction that amounts to roughly 17 percent. That difference may be just enough to help you buy the property you want.

However, notice the difference in the mortgages over the long term. With the fully amortized mortgage at the end of 30 years, you will owe zero—the mortgage will be fully paid off. With the interest-only loan at the end of the 30 years, you'll still owe the full $200,000. After all, all you've been doing is paying the interest. There's no equity return in an interest-only mortgage. (See Chapter 1 for an explanation of "equity return.")

TIP

Many lenders will combine an interest-only mortgage with a balloon payment. For example, the mortgage will be written as if it were for 30 years, but it will all come due and be payable within 3 or 5 years or some other short term. Here you get the benefits both of a lower monthly payment because you're paying only interest *and* a lower interest rate because you have a shorter term. On the other hand, unfortunately, you also combine the risks of both types of financing. Yet another variation is an interest-only mortgage combined with an ARM with an initial start rate that's reduced.

Method 5: Look for a Negatively Amortized Mortgage

Usually I tell people to "look out" for a negatively amortized mortgage. However, if you're clever and quick, you may be able to use it to your advantage in getting a lower payment.

Negative amortization means that the mortgage gets bigger, not smaller. You owe *more* at the end of the term than the amount you started with. How can such a thing happen?

The answer is that some of the interest you would otherwise pay each month is instead added to the loan itself. For example, you get a $300,000 30-year mortgage at 6 percent *interest only*. Your payments are $1,500 a month, interest only. But you tell the lender that you can't afford $1,500 a month. You can afford only $1,000 a month.

Okay, the lender says, then each month for the first three years, we'll only charge you $1,000 a month. But that remaining $500 in interest we'll add to your loan. At the *end of the first month,* you'll only pay $1,000. But your loan will now be raised to $300,500. And so on each month.

This will continue each month for three years: you make lower payments while the loan grows.

Like the sound of getting your payment cut by a third? But don't like the idea of ending up owing more than you borrowed?

TRAP

A negatively amortized mortgage is a trade-off between lower payments and a higher mortgage. Many consider it to be unsound economically. I suggest it as a viable option if it's the only way you can buy a property and then only if you need the loan for a short term (plan to refinance or sell).

There are some limitations to a negatively amortized mortgage. Generally, you must have better credit to get it. And normally the lender is allowed to increase the mortgage amount only up to 125 percent. Once that amount is reached, the negative amortization stops, and your payment jumps up to where it needs to be to fully pay off the loan. Hence, it's only a stop-gap kind of financing, and typically it is only offered for a few years—usually three to five.

Most borrowers opt for a negatively amortized mortgage only in a hot market. They figure they'll compensate for the increasing loan amount with the increasing property value. In a declining market, on the other hand, a negatively amortized mortgage can be the kiss of death.

Remember, in a negatively amortized mortgage there is no equity return. Far from it, instead there's equity loss.

Method 6: Look for a Seller to Carry Back Creative Paper

This option can work in any market. *But* you need to find a seller who will work with you. That means a seller who understands real estate financing (or is willing to learn) and who has the desire and the means to carry back paper, usually a second mortgage. (Check above for reasons sellers might want to finance your purchase.)

Remember, a seller can do almost *anything* when it comes to financing your purchase. The seller is not bound by Treasury Department rules, as are institutional lenders such as banks. Sellers aren't even bound by common sense!

Further, remember that everything in real estate is negotiable. The key to creative financing is to make an offer to a seller and then get that seller to accept it. The offer can be anything.

For example, here's a creative financing offer that I have used in the past that has worked: I agree to take over the seller's existing mortgage, which is possible with some Federal Housing Administration (FHA) and Department of Veterans Affairs (VA) loans. The seller agrees to give me an interest-only mortgage for the balance of the purchase price at market rate all due in three years but with *no payments*.

Yes, you heard right. The seller's second mortgage has no payments. Rather, it all comes due in three years plus interest. As a result, for three years my monthly payments are ridiculously low.

Perhaps an example will help.

The seller wants $200,000 for the property and currently owes $100,000 on an assumable loan. The seller's payments are $600 a month. You assume the seller's mortgage and begin making the seller's old $600-a-month payments. The seller gives you a second mortgage for $100,000 at 7 percent for three years with no payments (all due in three years). What are your total payments on the $200,000 property?

If you answered $600 a month you're right.

Of course, you've only got three years. At the end, you owe more than you borrowed because interest has been added on to the second mortgage. You've probably got to sell or refinance. Nevertheless, it's three years of low payments during which time anything can happen.

Why would a seller be so generous? Maybe the market's tight and he or she has to sell quickly because of a divorce, loss of employment, or anything else. Who knows what motivates a seller?

No, certainly not all or even most sellers will accept this type of offer. But some will.

Variations of this type of creative financing are endless. They include getting the seller to carry the entire purchase price (100 percent LTV loan), which means you put nothing down and have no monthly payments!

Or getting a small new institutional loan and having the seller carry the balance with no payments on a second mortgage.

The key is finding a seller with whom you can work. Often it's the case that the property has a problem that the seller can't solve, and, hence, he or she is willing to negotiate on financing to make an otherwise difficult sale.

TIP

Remember, sellers don't usually scrutinize credit reports and credit scores the way banks and institutional lenders do. Often a person with weak credit can still purchase with a low payment using creative seller financing.

Conclusion: You Can Afford a Mortgage

From what we've just seen:

1. Your down payment can be as little as zero.
2. You can get the closing costs rolled into the mortgage.
3. Seller financing can overcome credit problems.
4. Your payments can be almost anything.

It all depends on whether or not you're willing to deal with the consequences. Most of those require you to refinance or sell short term (or chance losing the property to foreclosure).

You can get a mortgage; you just have to be creative—and bold. (See Chapter 6 for details on financing discussed here.)

Your Other Options

But, what if you're not bold? What if you're not willing to risk everything on a short three- or five-year mortgage term? What if you're not able to negotiate terms with a seller? What if even if you could get a mortgage, you feel it's too risky for you?

If that's the case, read on. There are other alternatives.

Using Your Rent Money to Buy—the Lease-Option

W hat if instead of paying rent each month to a landlord, you could pay that same money each month toward the purchase of a home? You could live in the property and, within certain limits, fix it up just the way you like. And then, after a few years, it would be yours.

Does that sound like a good plan?

It's certainly possible, using a technique for purchasing real estate that's as old and established as the field itself. It's called a *lease-option*. Essentially the name says it all. You lease the property as a tenant. *But*, and this is the important part, you also get an option to buy it.

With a lease-option you control the property. It's up to you to decide if you want to buy it. When properly drawn, if the property goes up in value during your tenancy, you can exercise your option and get the profits without ever having had to get a mortgage or even take title.

Sound even better?

In this chapter we're going to look at the ins and outs of a lease-option—its many strong points and its weaknesses. We're going to see if it's the sort of thing that would work to quickly get you into a home of your own.

The Types of Buyers Who Should Get Lease-Options

A lease-option is available to anyone who wants to control real estate. It's been used by investors and home buyers for years. It's particularly useful for those who can't currently afford to buy a home but want to move into a particular property immediately and have the option of purchasing it in the future.

Advantages of a Lease-Option over a Purchase

- **A minimum amount of cash is involved.** Usually there's a month or two of rent up front, but sometimes there's as little as zero cash going into the deal.
- **The monthly payment amount is similar to what rent would normally be.** There may be an increase over what you pay each month for rent, but usually it is nowhere near the amount you'd have to pay if you were buying with a new mortgage.
- **There is little to no qualifying.** There's no bank or institutional lender involved. You have to work only with a seller.
- **You don't pay taxes, owner's insurance, or mortgage interest during the lease period.**
- **You can get out of the purchase.** At the end of the option period, if *you* decide *not* to buy, you simply walk away from the deal. The seller has no hold on you.

- **You get the profits if you buy.** Assuming you lock in a price, when you exercise the option a few years down the road, if the property has gone up in value, the profit is yours—not the seller's.
- **You can minimize the risks.** There are risks to using a lease-option, but while they can't be eliminated, they often can be held to a minimum.

How Lease-Options Work

It's actually very simple. You've certainly heard of a "lease" and very probably of an "option," which is frequently used in trading stocks. A "lease-option" incorporates the principles of both types of agreements.

The way it works is that you agree to lease a home from a seller for a period of time, typically anywhere from six months to three years.

The lease-option period can be virtually any length of time that both you and the seller agree upon. **TIP**

In addition, the seller agrees to sell you that home—that is, the seller agrees to give you the option to buy that home—any time during that lease period, usually for a set price. (Sometimes the seller will insist that the purchase price escalate on a scale tied to inflation, but that's not commonly done.)

Remember, it's up to you to decide whether or not you want to buy it—that's the option. It's *your* option (not the seller's) whether to buy at any time during the lease-option period. You can simply refuse to buy it if you so choose. But the seller cannot refuse to sell it to you under the terms of the deal if you decide to *exercise* your option—that is, if you decide to make the purchase.

A Higher Monthly Rent

Of course, there is a catch. Usually the seller will insist on a monthly payment that's higher than you'd otherwise pay if you were simply renting the property. For example, if the market rate for rent on the home were $1,000, the seller might insist on a monthly rent of $1,250.

Why the extra $250 in our example?

There are two ways to understand why sellers charge a higher-than-market rent for a lease-option. The first is to see that it's simply an inducement to make them go for the deal. From a seller's perspective, getting higher-than-market rent makes giving you a lease-option more worthwhile, as opposed to simply selling the property outright to a cash buyer or simply renting it to a tenant.

TIP Everything in real estate is negotiable. There's no rule that says that you must pay a seller more than market rate for rent. You could insist on and perhaps get a deal at the market rent, or even below, although that's unlikely.

The second way to understand why the rent is usually higher than market is to see how these agreements developed historically, which takes us back to the 1950s and 1960s when lease-options became very popular. Remember, back then 20 percent down payments were the rule. However, few buyers had that much cash.

So the seller would offer the buyer a lease-option with a slightly higher rent, and then the seller would credit that excess rent back to the buyer when the purchase was eventually made. In other words, the $250 extra a month wasn't lost—it was applied to the down payment on the property when it was bought.

Part of the Rent Goes toward the Purchase

Further, to help ensure that buyers could quickly accumulate the necessary down payment, sellers would add a bonus. They would apply not only that excess rent toward a down payment but some of the regular rent as well. In a deal such as the one described above, the seller might credit the buyer with $500 each month toward the down payment *if* and *when* the buyer went through with the purchase.

The incentive here was to keep the buyers on the hook as tenants paying higher-than-market rent and then give them a real reason to make the purchase once the lease-option expired.

Today, of course, with nothing-down financing, there is far less need for the seller's cash-back credit in order to make the sale. Nevertheless, the tradition endures. In most lease-options the seller will agree to credit you with a substantial portion of the rent, typically over and above the excess rent you'll be paying beyond market price. As we've seen, it would not be uncommon in our example to have on a market-rate rent of $1,000 a lease-option rental rate of $1,250 of which there would be a cash-back credit to you of $500 a month.

Keep in mind, however, that you get the credit *only if* you exercise the option and buy the property. If you do not buy the property at the end of the option period, you lose the cash-back credit.

TRAP

Therein lies one of the dangers with a lease-option. As we'll see, some unscrupulous sellers purposely pick tenant-buyers who they predict will not be able to make the eventual purchase because of financial reasons. Thus, these sellers get a higher-than-market rent for a few years, and when the tenant—would-be buyers can't make the purchase and have to move, the sellers get to keep it all . . . and do it again.

For you as a buyer, a lease-option can be a winning situation. Yes, you probably will have to pay an additional amount in rent. Yet all of the additional amount plus part of the regular rent will likely be returned to you as a credit when you make your eventual purchase.

You can use that credit toward a down payment or perhaps use it toward closing costs or in some cases, simply have it be returned to you as cash back out of the deal.

Lease-Option Example

Jason and Amber wanted to purchase a home, and they found a seller who was agreeable. The seller had an appraisal showing the home's then current value was $200,000. If Jason and Amber were to buy outright, their monthly payments (mortgage payment, taxes, and insurance) would run about $2,000 a month at then prevailing interest rates.

At the same time a similar home down the street was for rent, and the landlord was asking $1,250 a month. Thus, the monthly payment differential between renting and owning was $750 a month. (Remember, you can usually deduct taxes and interest from that monthly payment when you own, so the true differential was much less.)

However, Jason and Amber had a credit problem stemming from the previous year when they were both temporarily unemployed and missed a lot of payments. Unfortunately, they'd been told that because of their previous bad credit, they wouldn't qualify for the mortgage they needed to purchase the home.

So they decided to try a lease-option. Their rent would be $1,500 a month for three years. (That was $250 over market rate.) And the seller would credit them with $500 a month if and when they made the purchase. Over three years that would come to $18,000.

That was nearly three years ago, and they paid their rent regularly. In addition, they paid to have a new water heater put in when the original one burst. And they painted the house inside and out on their own.

Also, they strictly paid all their bills on time and reestablished excellent credit. Now they're ready to buy, and they've notified the seller that they intend to exercise their option. The seller has moved forward, and the house is now in escrow.

During the three years the home went up in value from $200,000 to $231,525. That's an increase of 5 percent a year (the historical average), or $31,525 more than their option requires them to pay. They'll be getting the benefit of that price increase, not the seller.

Further, the seller will credit them with $18,000 ($500 monthly) from the three years' rent they paid during the time they lived in the home. Since they are getting a 100 percent LTV loan, the credit is in the form of hard money. They'll use $8,000 to cover their closing costs and take the rest back in cash. Their deal looks like this:

Home Purchase by Exercising the Option

Current home value	$231,525
Purchase price as agreed on in option	200,000
Automatic equity to Jason and Amber	$ 31,525
New 100 percent mortgage	$200,000
Credit from seller from rent	+18,000
Closing costs	− 8,000
Cash back to buyers Jason and Amber	$ 10,000

Note that upon the close of escrow, Jason and Amber will have an automatic equity in their property of over $31,000. Further, they will get cash back of $10,000 (after paying costs of purchase) to do with as they wish. They have *no* out-of-pocket expenses.

On the negative side, they did pay an extra $250 a month over the normal rent. However, that was three years earlier. During that time rents in the neighborhood have moved up. Today, a rent of $1,500 would no longer be considered excessive.

Further, the way their lease-option was written, they were responsible for minor maintenance, and that meant they had to replace a water heater and paint the home. But if they had owned the home during those years, those would be their normal expenses anyhow. Note that in many lease-options, the owner-seller will handle all repairs and maintenance, just as in a regular tenancy. However, typically in those cases the rent is higher. Further, you may want to insist on a professional inspection of the property before entering into the lease-option so you'll have a better idea of what you're getting yourself into. Finally, if repairs become costly, say an oil furnace needs to be replaced, you should negotiate the cost with the owner-seller—after all, it's still his or her property. You certainly don't want to pay for costly repairs and then end up not buying the home!

Advantages Amber and Jason Got from the Lease-Option

1. They locked in a purchase price three years before they actually bought. That gave them an automatic equity in the property at the time of the purchase.
2. They locked in a rental rate and avoided rent increases that regular tenants had to face.
3. A significant portion of their rent was credited back to them so that they received cash back when they purchased.
4. During the three-year term of the lease-option, for the most part they were able to treat the property as their own.

Advantages of Lease-Options for Sellers

After going through this example, I'm sure many readers are wondering why a seller would want to give a buyer a lease-option. Why give up all of that profit? Why credit back so much of the rent? Wouldn't a seller be crazy to do such a thing?

Actually, when properly handled, a lease-option can be a win-win deal for both buyer and seller. Here are the advantages to a seller in agreeing to a lease-option with you.

- **The seller is having trouble selling the home and is faced with a monthly mortgage payment.** Having a lease-option in place virtually guarantees money coming in each month to cover the mortgage, and there's a probable sale down the road.

- **The seller is a reluctant landlord who has had bad experiences with tenants (they've run off without paying the rent, made a mess of the place, refused to leave or pay, and on and on).** A lease-option can almost guarantee that the tenants will pay the rent each month at a higher-than-market rate, they will probably act responsibly since this will soon be their home, and depending on how the lease-option is structured, they may even take care of minor maintenance.

- **It's an almost sure sale, which can be important if it's a tight market.** The difference between a lease-option and an outright sale is time—even though the seller has to wait to get his or her money, the seller still usually gets a sale.

- **The selling price is locked in.** Yes, prices might go up during the lease-option period (in which case the seller would lose), but prices might also stagnate or even go down. With a lease-option, the seller knows what he or she is going to get for the property. And in some cases it may be possible to tag an automatic inflation increase onto the price (see below).

- **It can be a headache relief.** Many people want to get rid of a property simply because it's a distraction from a bigger problem they might have, which could be job loss, divorce, illness, forced retirement, or something else. (This might turn into a problem for you the buyer, as we'll see shortly.) They don't want to bother putting the house on the market, and they certainly don't want the usual trials and tribulations of being a landlord. A lease-option can (hopefully) offer them a painless way to ease out of ownership.

Every day in most states of the country, buyer and seller nego-
tiated lease-options are win-win situations for everyone involved.
They can be a plus for the buyer and a plus for the seller.

TRAP

Because of abuses of the lease-option (discussed below) by some unscrupulous
sellers, some states (such as Texas) have virtually outlawed the tool. Be sure you
check with a good agent and/or attorney in your state before proceeding to work
on a lease-option.

Potential Problems with Lease-Options

We've seen the advantages of the lease-option. Now let's look at
some of the potential weaknesses more closely.

The Buyer's Being Unable to Buy

It's important at the onset to realize that a lease-option is definitely
not a purchase. You do *not* get title to the property. Rather, you get
a lease and an option to purchase down the road.

When it comes time to exercise that option, it's up to you to
come up with the purchase money. In our example, that means
coming up with $200,000.

To do this, presumably, you'd go out and get financing from an
institutional lender such as a bank. You'd get up to a 100 percent
LTV mortgage, or if you desired, put some cash into the property
as a down payment and get a lower LTV loan. (The seller's cash-
back credit would help here.)

However, there's no guarantee that three years down the road
(or however long your option period is for) you will be able to
qualify for a mortgage. Financial conditions can change quickly, as
they did in 2007 with the breakdown of the subprime mortgage
market. Interest rates may be higher, making it more difficult to
qualify. The type of mortgage you want may simply not be

available anymore. Or you might be out of work, or you might have had to move into a lower-paying position at work.

One of the risks you take with a lease-option is that you just might not be able to get the mortgage you need to make the purchase when you need it.

How to Minimize the Risk. There's no way to eliminate this risk completely; however, it can be minimized in the following three ways.

1. **You can get preapproved today.** *For virtually nothing,* a mortgage broker can tell you at the time you get the lease-option just how likely you are to qualify for a mortgage to make a purchase. In our example with Jason and Amber, the mortgage broker explained that they would qualify *if* they had several uninterrupted years of good credit. Feeling that they could accomplish this, they went ahead. *Of course, there are no guarantees. The market will surely change over a period of years and having qualified before, doesn't mean they'll qualify later. This is simply a good indicator to consider.*

2. **You can ask to have the option extended.** Before the option period expires, if you realize you're not going to be able to get a needed mortgage, you can go back to the seller and ask for an extension. The seller may or may not grant this, depending on his or her own financial needs and desires. However, you can often sweeten the pot by agreeing to pay a higher price for the property and increased rent. Many sellers will be agreeable, although there are certainly no guarantees. (An automatic extension can be written into the option, but most sellers will not go along with this.)

3. **You can plan on moving.** Understanding that the lease-option is a risk for you means that if worst comes to

worst, you may have to simply walk away from the property. Of course, the only thing that you will actually lose is the higher-than-market rent you may have paid.

TRAP

In some cases the seller will demand separate option money—perhaps a thousand dollars or more—for the option portion of the deal. This, however, tends to be rare, and usually the increased rent is considered the option money, and no additional funds are required on your part.

If you can't get a mortgage with which to buy the property by the time the option expires, you could lose. It is a risk.

The Seller's Being Unwilling to Honor the Option

This is rare; however, in the booming market of the early 2000s, it happened more frequently than it had in the past. The time would come for the buyers to exercise the option. They would obtain a commitment for the necessary new mortgage and would open escrow. And then the seller would simply refuse to sign the deed over to them.

How can the seller refuse? After all, he or she signed a lease-option that was intended to be a legally binding document. Won't there be serious legal consequences to the seller by refusing? Probably, but . . .

It usually happens like this. You get an option to buy a particular property for $250,000 three years in the future. However, during the intervening years, the real estate prices go through the roof. When the time comes for you to exercise the option, the property is worth $600,000. To sell to you at $250,000, the seller would take a $350,000 loss. That's a lot of money.

Some unscrupulous sellers will instead simply decide to stonewall it. They'll refuse to sell. At that point, your only recourse is to hire an attorney and have the lease-option adjudicated.

You'll have to go to court. That will cost you time and money. And depending on how a judge sees the lease-option you might win, or not. Nothing is for certain.

Another way this situation might play out is that the seller might come to you and say something like, "Let's compromise. I'll sell the property to you for $400,000. That's still $200,000 below market—all profit to you. But I'll also get to share some of the equity increase the property saw during the last few years."

To avoid a lengthy and costly lawsuit, would you agree?

How to Minimize the Risk. Again, there's no way to eliminate the risk of this happening, rare though it might be. But you can minimize it by taking the following precautions.

1. **Know the person with whom you're dealing.** An honest person doesn't usually turn dishonest. If the person selling the property was honest when you got the lease-option, he or she is likely to stay so. This is one of several reasons (others are below) that I suggest you get a credit report on the seller before going through with the lease-option. (The seller will surely want one on you, so just return the favor.) Someone with excellent credit is more likely to be a straight shooter.

2. **Insert an automatic price increase into the lease-option.** This is not as commonly done, but it's not unusual. It's a phrase that an attorney or a good agent can put in that says the price you'll pay will go up, say, 3 percent a year. Or the increase could be tied to inflation or housing prices in the area. Having such a clause in the lease-option accomplishes two things: It takes away the feeling from the seller that he or she isn't participating in profit taking, so there's less incentive to stonewall. And if things should ever get to court, it spells out the profit the seller has already agreed to.

3. **Keep tracking the market, and act in a timely way.** Finally, keep in mind that although it did happen in the early 2000s, the likelihood of the market again doubling or even tripling within a few years is exceedingly unlikely. However, it could happen, in any given region, for example, so you should follow market prices closely. (For clues on how to do this, see Chapter 2.) If prices suddenly start accelerating, consider immediately exercising your option. (Remember, you can exercise the option *any time* prior to its expiration.) You're far less likely to get an agitated seller trying to stonewall you if the price of the property has gone up 25 percent, than if it has gone up 250 percent.

Yes, the seller might refuse to honor the option. But there could be serious legal ramifications for the seller if he or she does that. Few sellers will try. In any event, it's an excellent reason to have the lease-option drawn up or at the least approved by your attorney.

The Seller's Loss of the Property

This is a serious problem and one that has received a lot of attention in recent years, particularly in some states in the Southwest. In Texas, lease-options have been severely restricted in the sense that the seller must have a very large equity in the property.

When you buy a property outright, there is a short period of time called an *escrow* when the seller comes up with the deed to the property. There's a title search to see what the seller owes and to be sure all the seller's liens (mortgages and other debts) are paid off (unless you assume them). And you get a clear title to the home. You obtain title insurance, which assures you that the property is yours.

When you buy on a lease-option, none of that happens, at least not initially. There is no escrow, no title insurance, no title change, and no payoff of the seller's debt. Instead, you are simply given a document—a lease-option—that spells out your lease period and terms and specifies the conditions under which you have the right to exercise your option to purchase at a later date.

However, what if the seller is having serious financial problems? What if she finds that because of a job loss, illness, divorce, or any of a hundred other possible problems, she can't make the monthly payment on her mortgage? So she stops making it.

The mortgage company is not happy about not getting paid, so it accelerates the mortgage, making it all due and payable—foreclosure. It eventually takes the property back. Where does that leave you?

Once foreclosure is complete and the mortgage company has ownership of the property, your seller is out of the picture. She can no longer honor your option even if she wanted to. Your chances of buying the property could be out the window, along with any cash-back credit of your rent the seller was intending to give you.

Of course, you could deal directly with the mortgage company. They certainly don't want the property, and perhaps you could buy it from them. And then again, perhaps not.

Or it could play out in a different way. Your seller could keep making the mortgage payments. But she could get herself in all kinds of debt, and her creditors could start slapping liens on the property in an attempt to get their money back. It wouldn't take very long before there were more liens on the home than it might be worth. Were you to exercise your option, you might suddenly find that the seller is *upside down*—that is, she owes more on the house than the price you've agreed to.

A seller who is in financial difficulty is not one from whom you want to get a lease-option. Even if the seller wants to sell you the property, it can turn out that when you eventually exercise the option, she may be in such financial straits that she can't comply with it.

TRAP

Some states now require that before a seller can give a lease-option, he or she must own the property free and clear, or very near to it. The idea is that that seller must be in a financial position to be able to go through with the option portion of the deal. Check with a good agent or attorney in your area to see what the local rules are.

This previously rare problem has become more acute in recent years because of the actions of some unscrupulous speculators. They have bought properties themselves using a variety of financial devices (including the lease-option). Once they gain control of the home, they then rent it out for the maximum rent, achieved largely through the use of the lease-option given to unwary tenants-buyers. They collect the rent but sometimes make no payments on the mortgage. They may be able to control the property and collect rents for a year or more before the lender finally forecloses or the original seller takes the property back. From that point on, the speculators are out of the picture. And all your money, as well as your option, could be lost.

As before, you can't really eliminate the risk. But here's how you can minimize it.

How to Minimize the Risk

1. **Find out how long the seller has owned the property.** You can ask. But even more important, you can have your agent (or you can do this on your own) get a quick title search. (A *condition of title report* is usually available at minimal cost.) If your seller obtained control of the property only yesterday or if the title is actually in someone else's name and your seller is simply a middleman, it's a red flag. Time to bail out. You want to see your seller's name in black and white on the title, and you want to see

that he or she has sizable equity in the property before you get into a lease-option.

2. **Get a credit report on the seller.** As noted above, the seller will surely get one on you, and believing that what's good for the goose is likewise good for the gander, there should be no problem in your getting one on him or her. Any agent should be able to run this for you. You want a seller with impeccable credit, or at least credit as good as yours. The better the credit, the less likely the seller will get into financial trouble and lose the property.

3. **Read all the notices that come to the house.** Frequently the first time you, or the seller, are aware that there's a financial problem is when a lender or other creditor sends a notice. (The notices usually state what they are right on the envelope.) Even if the seller has requested mail forwarding, these notices still somehow have a way of coming right through. If one arrives addressed to the seller, don't just forward it to him or her. Take it to the seller personally and ask for an explanation. You have a right to know if the seller is in financial trouble. Maybe you'll want to try and exercise your option immediately. Maybe you can work out a better deal for you with the seller right on the spot.

When you get a lease-option, you're counting on the financial health of the seller. If that health is impaired, he or she may not be able to convey title to you when you want, or he or she may lose the home even before the end of the option period. This is possibly the most serious threat you may face, and you should take steps to minimize it.

The Seller's Selling the Property to Someone Else

You shouldn't be dealing with this kind of seller. He's an outright crook. He gives you a lease-option. And then, after a few months, he attempts to sell the property to another buyer, thus cutting you completely out of the deal and in some states, breaking the law.

How could such an unscrupulous person pull this off?

Remember, with a lease-option you get a document, not a deed. You don't get title to the property until you exercise that option, usually some years later. In the meantime, all you've got is a lease-option—a piece of paper.

If the seller can somehow manage to bamboozle another buyer into thinking that he can sell the property unimpaired, he might go through with the sale including the title search and even transfer of title and title insurance to the new buyer!

TRAP

Obtaining a standard title insurance policy does not usually involve having anyone physically check out the property to see that the house is there or to see if there's a tenant or someone else who might have an unrecorded interest, such as a lease-option. (Title insurance may, however, protect the unwary buyer against unrecorded documents such as your lease-option.) Buying a special extended form of title insurance called a *lender's title insurance policy* [also known as an *American Land Title Association* (ALTA) *lender's policy*], does usually involve the insurer sending someone out to check for these things.

No, most sellers would not be this unscrupulous. Nevertheless, you should do what you can to minimize the chances of this happening.

How to Minimize the Risk. Record a copy of the lease-option agreement. Sometimes called a *memorandum of lease-option,* you may be able to record this document. When you record a lease-option, it gives constructive notice to everyone that you have an interest in the property. Any buyer with common sense (not all have that, unfortunately!) will want a title search and title insurance, and the title search will reveal your option.

No, recording the option probably won't prevent a determined owner from giving someone else a deed, but it might do the next best thing—alert the prospective buyer to a problem and prevent him or her from getting title insurance. That's often enough to keep a deal from being consummated.

The problem is that in some areas it's difficult to record the lease-option agreement. There can be many reasons, but the most common is that many recording offices will accept only those documents on which everyone's signature has been notarized. Since the seller may refuse to have his or her signature notarized, you may have trouble recording the document. (Some states now allow documents to be recorded where only one signature has been notarized, which in this case could be yours.)

TIP

Title transfers and all matters affecting the title to a property are normally recorded with the respective county, township, or other similar entity. Lenders, buyers, and others rely on this recording procedure to determine who owns a property and who has interests in it. Often recording a document is the best way to ensure that your interest in a property is protected. The rule is that the document recorded first has precedence.

Although recording a memorandum of your lease-option may go a long way toward protecting you, it could also land you in hot water with the legitimate rights of the owner—see below.

The Seller's Further Encumbering the Property

Remember that with a lease-option, you don't own the property. The seller retains ownership rights until you exercise that option and the title is transferred to you. One of those ownership rights is right to refinance.

The seller may wish to refinance the property while you're living there in order to get a lower interest rate, lower payments, or to pull money out. This is certainly within his or her rights.

Your concern is that the seller not get a mortgage on the property for more than the agreed selling price because the seller's higher mortgage will make it difficult if not impossible for you to buy the property under your option. For example, you could be in trouble if you've agreed to buy for $200,000 and the seller refinances to a new loan of $250,000. Now the seller owes more on the property than the amount for which he or she has agreed to sell it to you. When it comes time to exercise your option, the seller might not be able to perform.

TIP

In some states encumbering the property over the option amount is considered illegal.

Once again, you cannot totally eliminate this risk. But you can minimize it.

How to Minimize the Risk

1. **Insert a clause in the lease-option dealing with seller refinancing.** No seller would likely agree to a clause that prohibited his or her refinancing. However, it would not be unreasonable to ask the seller to restrict any refinancing to an amount not greater than the agreed-upon price. (Keep in mind, however, that this would be part of a contract that would probably be enforceable by you only if you decided to hire a lawyer and take it to court.)

2. **Record a copy of your lease-option.** As noted above, this should have the effect of giving lenders notice that you have an interest in the property. Presumably in order for the seller to refinance, you'd have to sign some sort of release that would give you some veto power over the amount and type of financing that the seller could arrange.

As you can see, the lease-option is not a panacea; it does offer some challenges. I wouldn't rely on a lease-option prepared entirely by the seller. Before entering into it, you'd be wise to consult with a good real estate agent and attorney to be sure it's written properly and your rights are protected. Many attorneys who specialize in real estate will do this for a nominal fee.

Finding Lease-Option Sellers

If after going through the pros and cons of lease-options you'd like to pursue the matter further, how do you begin? The answer is that you need to find a seller who might be interested in having a lease-option with you.

While you'll certainly want to have a good attorney draw up the lease-option document for you (or at least approve the one the seller may want to use), your first big step is going to be to find an agreeable seller. Remember, most sellers want to cash out their property—they want a sale now, rather than later. And most want the money to buy another property. But not all.

As we noted earlier, there are many reasons that sellers might want to have a lease-option on their property (to ensure a sale in a tight market, remove a headache, get out from under a rental, and so on, as we mentioned earlier in the chapter). The question now becomes, how do you find these particular sellers?

TIP

Remember that location is always important in real estate—not only as protection for the value of your property but also to get you into a neighborhood with the level of safety, quality of schools, and size and type of house you want. Be sure to look first for a lease-option seller in those areas where you most want to live. Don't be tempted to move to a distant or undesirable neighborhood just by the lure of a lease-option.

Here are some avenues to investigate when looking for a lease-option seller.

- **Check newspaper ads.** This may seem bonehead simple, but it's often the quickest and easiest way to find the sellers with whom you want to negotiate. Most sellers who are willing to give a lease-option will advertise the fact. Look both in the "for rent" and the "for sale" sections of the paper, and look for small ads, perhaps just a couple of lines. Just remember, however, that using newspaper ads will most likely lead you to dealing directly with the seller and not with a seller's agent, so you'll need to be prepared to carry the ball yourself. (See below about how to deal with an agent for a lease-option.)

- **Check the Internet.** Use the key words "lease option." There are literally hundreds of sites across the country that either discuss or offer lease-option opportunities.

- **Check flyers.** Creative sellers know that the most expensive advertising is in newspapers. Hence, they look for alternatives. One of the best alternative methods of reaching a potential tenant-buyer is to post flyers in prominent locations. These locations can be supermarkets, drugstores, even telephone poles. Usually the flyers are made with little tear-off tags at the bottom that give the seller's phone number. Give the seller a call. Yes, it may be a dead end, or you might just locate a winner.

- **Check housing offices.** You can check with local industries and larger employers, schools, churches, and any other places in your community that offer help in finding housing. Often you do not need to be a member of the organization to use the housing office. Sometimes notices will simply be posted on bulletin boards outside the offices. This can be an excellent source because relatively few people outside the organizations take advantage of it.

- **Try to find for-sale-by-owner (FSBO) sellers.** These are sellers who are trying to circumvent the agents by selling on their own. You should be aware that many, perhaps most, of these sellers give up before they find a buyer. By contacting them, you can give them hope and an alternative. They may be very receptive to a lease-option. However, be prepared to explain what a lease-option is. Remember too that an FSBO seller has a mindset aimed at an outright sale. Now you're asking him or her to go in a different direction so you might encounter some initial hesitation.

You can find FSBOs by checking your local newspaper under "homes for sale." Look for "by owner" ads. Also, try simply touring the streets of the neighborhoods where you want to live and looking for FSBO signs. Then if you see an FSBO property you are interested in, you can send the seller a letter describing what you want. Or—and this is a method I prefer—call and ask. The seller's number is almost always on the sign. If the seller's agreeable, stop by and discuss the idea.

- **Try scrounging.** There are lots of sellers who would like to dispose of their property anyway they can, but they simply aren't actively working at selling. When you're touring a neighborhood, look for vacant homes. Perhaps there's an out-of-town owner who'd love to give you a lease-option. An owner's name can be found by checking with a local service found in most communities that will give you the name and address of the person who pays the taxes on the property. Or you can simply send a letter to the property address marked to be forwarded to the owner. Chances are the post office will deliver your note for you.

- **Convert a rental.** Look for landlords who are offering to rent property. When you find a home you like, offer a lease-option. Many landlords will be tempted. I know I would be if a would-be tenant turned out to be a would-be buyer!

- **Talk it up.** Tell everyone you meet what you are looking for. I once bought a home from a person I met who happened to be sitting in a seat next to me on a plane in which I was traveling. I struck up a conversation, and lo and behold, he was looking to sell just what I wanted! You never know.

Dealing with Agents

This can be both easier and more difficult. It's easier because presumably the agent knows exactly what you want and can direct you to just the right seller. The agent can also handle all the paperwork.

It's more difficult because you're telling the agent that he or she will have to wait years before he or she gets the commission. As a result the agent may be disinclined to help you.

What you need to do is find an agent who is willing to work with you. After all, you are a buyer. It's just that your purchase won't be consummated right away.

Finding the Right Agent

My suggestion is that you spend some time interviewing agents. Often agents who handle rentals can be your best source. After all, they deal day in and day out with sellers who are landlords and who may be very interested in having a lease-option.

You can create a list of agents from the following sources.

Creating an Agent List

- If you know a friend who's in the business, talk to him or her. There are well over a million licensed agents in this country, so chances are excellent that nearly everyone knows someone who knows at least one.

- Get recommendations from friends, relatives, and associates. If someone can recommend an agent with whom they recently worked, this is a big plus.
- Check the neighborhoods where you want to live for agents' signs. As soon as a house is listed, the agent puts up a sign. This not only advertises the house but also the agent. Usually there's one agent, or maybe two, who dominate an area. Talk to them.
- If all else fails, use the Yellow Pages of the phone book. But be sure to look for an agent who's local to the area where you want to live. You do not want an agent whose work area is distant from your desired location.

Interviewing the Agent

You want an agent who is willing and able to work for you. That means not only that the agent will look for lease-option sellers but also that the agent is competent. I suggest asking the agent the following questions.

Questions to Ask an Agent

- **"Will you work to help me find a seller who will give me a lease-option?"** Many agents will not because they're interested only in immediate sales. Better to find this out sooner than later. A simple yes or no now should tell you.
- **"How much time can you give to me?"** Be point blank. Is the agent willing to work the hours it will take to help you find a lease-option seller?
- **"Do you handle rentals?"** Most agents do not as their major line of work. Rather, they specialize in listings (that is, he or she is a *lister*) or they deal with buyers and sellers. Getting an agent who handles rentals can be a good step up for you.

- **"Do you work in the neighborhoods where I'm looking?"** Remember, you want a local agent. The local agent knows the houses, the sellers, and the past sales, and he or she can usually give you the best service.
- **"Can we work the near expireds?"** These are listings that are about to expire, usually around 90 days old. The agent can cull these from all the others. Often sellers who have had little success in a direct sale may be interested in a lease-option.
- **"How long have you been in business?"** I know it's unfair to those just starting out, but I prefer to do business with an old-timer, someone who's learned the ropes and isn't learning on me. I usually insist on dealing with an agent who has at least five years' experience.
- **"Are you a Realtor?"** The term *agent* is generic. The term *Realtor* refers to a member of the National Association of Realtors (NAR), the largest trade group in the country. It works to uphold the highest standards of service to clients. Why not work with the best?
- **"Can you provide references?"** Any agent worth his or her salt can and should be eager to do this. A list of satisfied buyers, sellers, and/or lessees should be proffered.

TIP

Broker refers to an agent or Realtor who has a license to buy, sell, lease, or option property and collect a commission. A *salesperson* is usually a beginning agent who must work under the auspices of a broker.

Handling the Commission

An agent isn't going to help you out of the goodness of his or her heart. An agent expects to get paid. And that can be a problem with a lease-option.

Consider a lease-option from an agent's point of view: An agent has a home listed for $200,000. When the property sells outright, the agent will get a good portion of a 6 percent commission. First the commission is usually split in half between the office representing the buyer and the office representing the seller. Then it's split again between the salesperson and the broker. Even though the seller may pay a 6 percent commission, the average real estate salesperson only gets about 1.5 percent. On a $200,000 home, the total commission would be $12,000 of which the agent with whom you deal may get only $3,000.

Nonetheless, that's $3,000 in cash, immediately.

On a lease-option, the sale may not be consummated for two to three years. The agent has to wait that length of time to get the money.

TIP

The seller usually pays the agent an immediate fee for obtaining a lease-option, and that fee is usually equal to the rent for one or two months. This fee, however, also has to be split between the broker and the salesperson and sometimes between offices.

What should be evident is that to the agent, an outright sale is going to be much more profitable than a lease-option—hence the reluctance to work with you.

On the other hand, if the house hasn't sold and the listing is about to expire and the agent realizes that he or she may not get any commission at all, then a lease-option is better than nothing. That's why it's often best to work with agents on near-expired listings.

How to Get the Agent More Involved

One way to pique the agent's interest is to pay a part of the commission up front. You can sweeten the lease-option by telling the agent that you'll come up with, for example, 1.5 percent (or 3 percent, but never more than that) of the future sales price, right now, in cash. Of course, when the house eventually sells, you'll have the seller credit you with the amount you've already paid the agent, and that has to be written into the lease-option.

The advantage is that you remove the money obstacle that the agent has to working with you. You provide the incentive to get the agent working hard, quickly.

On the other hand, it's going to cost you money out of pocket. On a $200,000 house, 1.5 percent is $3,000 up front. Yes, you'll get it back *if* you exercise your option and buy the property. But that's a long way down the road. And if you don't eventually buy the property, you'll lose your money.

Is it worthwhile to pay a portion of the agent's commission up front? It all depends on how badly you need a good agent working for you. Remember, agents handle nearly 90 percent of all properties listed. They work day in and day out with sellers. And they are without question your single best source of finding a suitable lease-option seller. Plus, they usually will throw in all the lease-option paperwork in exchange for the up-front fee.

It's something to seriously consider.

Lease-Purchases

A lease-purchase is a variation of the lease-option. Here, however, you don't get the option of buying. Rather, you commit to a purchase.

With a *lease-purchase*, you agree to rent the property for a period of time. However, you also agree to then purchase it according to the terms of your contract. Usually the price and other terms of the sale are agreed to at the time the lease-purchase is obtained.

Keep in mind that here you can't at some point simply say you don't want to buy the property. With a lease-purchase contract, you sign an agreement to purchase at the end of your tenancy.

The seller would be within his or her rights to take you to court if you tried to walk away from the deal.

This is, of course, nothing other than a delayed purchase. And note that lease-purchases may actually be restricted or the term may be limited in certain states; you need to verify with your attorney and/or agent the particular laws in your state before you enter into this type of agreement. The only reason you'd want to use a lease-purchase is if you decided you absolutely must have the house and the seller was refusing to give you a lease-option. You might say, "Okay, then, I'll buy it. But I can't buy it until the end of a year or two, during which time I'll lease it." A seller who didn't want to deal with the uncertainty of a lease-option might feel a whole lot better about a lease-purchase. (See also *land contracts of sale* in Chapter 5.)

Transferring Lease-Options

One of the conditions you may want to insist upon in your lease-option is the right to transfer it. That means that if you decide not to exercise the option for whatever reason, you can transfer it to someone else who will exercise it. For example, after two and a half years of a three-year lease-option, you realize that you can't qualify for a needed mortgage. So you transfer your option to another person—a buyer—who can go through with the deal.

Why would you want the right to do this?

It's an important escape valve for you, and it can save you money. For example, suppose you were nearing the end of your option period when you realize that you can't or don't want to purchase the home. If you simply walk away at the end of the lease, you lose all of the rent money (including any excess rent amount) that you've paid. But if at that point you transfer your option to a third party, you may be able to recapture some or even all of that money.

This is particularly the case if the value of the property has gone up during the option period. Why give that new equity in the property back to the seller? Simply find a buyer for the property and transfer your option to him or her. Now the new buyer gets the benefit of some of that new equity. And you get some of your rent money back.

Will a seller accept a transfer clause?

Probably. After all, it's not the big thing to ask for that it may first sound like. You could probably exercise your option and then immediately resell to someone else anyhow. Here, you're simply saying that instead of entering into a purchase and a sale, you simply want to effect a transfer. Having this clause can save you some closing costs and make concluding a deal much easier. (There may also be some tax advantages—see your accountant.)

TIP

In exercising an option and then quickly reselling (in essence flipping) a property, most lease-optionees run two escrows that close simultaneously. In one, you exercise the option and get the title. And then immediately in the other, you transfer that title to your buyer. You own the property for only a theoretical moment in time. Escrow companies are familiar with this and handle it all the time. However, keep in mind that depending on how these are structured, in some cases double escrowing is not only unethical but is also illegal. Be sure you contact a good attorney to make the deal for you, and make sure that all parties know what's happening because hiding some information could get you into trouble.

Lease-Option Opportunities under Section 8

If part or all of your rent is being paid by the state under Section 8 (rent payments for low-income housing), you may now be able to enter into a lease-option. Contact the state office where you live for the exact details in your area.

This type of contract would work virtually the same as it would for any other lease-option. The only difference is that some of the lease money comes from the state and not you.

Many sellers are delighted to do a lease-option under Section 8. After all, the chances of the rent being sent on time every month by the state are much higher than for almost any other tenant.

The Bottom Line

Is a lease-option for you?

It's not for everyone. But it can provide a reasonably quick and easy way for you to get on the road to homeownership. After all, why not use your rent money as part of a purchase rather than let it simply be wasted on endless rent?

If you're

- Low on cash
- Have credit problems
- Can't qualify for a mortgage
- Or otherwise need a creative solution to purchasing a home

then you should consider a lease-option. It's not a panacea. But it can make a huge difference for many people.

Contract-for-Sale or Subject-To Purchases

Here are two techniques that have worked for thousands of renters in the past. They can allow you to purchase real estate without paying much more than your monthly rental payment. They are ways to get into property when you don't have a lot of cash and you can't afford high payments. Indeed, the monthly payments are often a fraction of what they would be were you to purchase the home outright. They may even be less than you're currently paying for rent!

However, be aware that these techniques are not without risks, as we'll see shortly.

Contract-for-Sale Purchases

These work like layaway sales. Think of it in this fashion: You want to buy a particular TV. But you don't have enough cash. So you go to the store and arrange to buy the set on a "layaway plan," which means that you'll pay the store so much money each month until you reach the price the TV set was selling for the day you began your layaway payments, at which point you'll get the set.

A contract for sale is similar. You enter into a contract to purchase a home from a seller. You do not get a deed. You do not get a title. You get a contract to buy. When you've paid an agreed-upon amount to the seller, you can purchase the property, usually subject to your getting financing.

TIP

In different regions of the country, this device is known by a variety of names including these:

- Installment sales contract
- Land contract of sale
- Agreement (or contract) for purchase and sale
- Agreement to convey

Keep in mind, however, that *unlike* a layaway plan, you *do* normally get to move into the property. And your monthly payments don't have to eventually equal the purchase price. Rather, you pay the price down until you can go out and finance the remainder of the purchase.

For example, you'll pay $1,000 a month for five years accumulating $60,000. This is subtracted from a purchase price of $350,000, and you go out and get a mortgage for the balance of $290,000.

Typically you'll handle all maintenance and upkeep. And you'll move in. If after the five years in our example, you've kept up the payments and you obtain the needed financing to pay off the purchase price, the seller gives you the title.

Does that sound like a lease-option? It's not the same. Here there's no lease. You're not a tenant. And the option to walk away if you decide not to purchase doesn't exist. You agree to buy the home, in our example, when the contract is made.

At the same time the seller agrees to sell to you. You have what's intended to be a legally binding contract.

Why Would I Want a Contract for Sale?

Basically, a contract for sale skirts the issues of financing and title transfer, at least until you actually conclude the purchase. You don't have to get a mortgage. You don't pay any closing costs such as escrow fees or title insurance. And your monthly payment is whatever you and the seller agree upon, and as noted, that's often a lot less than it would cost to get a mortgage.

Advantages to the Buyer in a Contract-for-Sale Agreement

- There's no financing involved.
- You get to move in immediately.
- There are no closing costs.
- You often have very low monthly payments.

Historically, this was a method that someone who wanted to buy farmland used to make the purchase. The buyer would live on the land and farm it while paying the seller a monthly fee. Eventually, after a number of years, if the buyer kept up the payments, the seller would sign the deed over.

Today it works the same for homes.

Keep in mind, however, that when it comes time to purchase, you usually haven't paid the full price. You still need to get a new mortgage to come up with the full amount that you originally agreed upon with the seller. That usually will necessitate a significant bump in monthly payments.

Why Would a Seller Want to Give Me a Contract for Sale?

The single biggest reason that sellers have historically used a contract for sale is the ease with which they could eliminate your interest in the property *if* you failed to keep up the monthly payments. If you don't make the payments, you're out. Years ago this meant that some unscrupulous sellers would institute "self-help evictions"—they would bodily throw the buyers out of the property.

Today, of course, to get any reluctant buyers out, the sellers must go to court and prove a default on the contract. Nevertheless, because many contracts for sale are unrecorded, in these situations, the buyer has fewer protections than he or she would have in an outright subject-to purchase (see below).

TRAP

In actual practice, when buyers stop making the payments on a contract for sale, they already see the writing on the wall and usually soon leave of their own accord. Sellers are aware of this and rely on its happening some of the time.

Advantages to the Seller in a Contract-for-Sale Agreement

- It makes it easier for the seller to eliminate a buyer's interest and get the property back.
- It can be an opportunity to sell in a slow market.
- It can quickly generate monthly income from the property.

What Are the Requirements for a Contract for Sale?

Generally speaking, the actual requirements are few. You and the seller must agree on the amount of the monthly payment. If the seller has owned the property for a long time, she may have a small mortgage on it with small mortgage and tax payments. She may agree to allow you to pay just enough to cover her payments. Hence, the monthly payment may actually end up being less than you're paying in rent.

You must also agree on a price that you'll eventually pay for the property and how long the contract is for. With real property, the only restriction usually is that the contract must be for a year or longer.

The document itself is fairly simple and short, and any good attorney can draw it up for you, often for a minimal fee. Some real estate agents can provide you with prepared forms, but you should take these to an attorney anyway who can make the language specific to your needs.

What Are the Risks for a Contract for Sale?

The main risk to the buyer comes from the fact that you may not have *recorded* title to the property. The seller retains the title and ownership until such time as you fulfill your contract and make the purchase. From this come other risks as well.

1. The seller, since he or she has the title to the property, can refinance and get a new mortgage above the amount for which you've agreed to purchase the property. That means when it comes time to buy, the seller might owe more than the purchase price. As a result, the seller might not be able to sell to you at the agreed-upon price, even if he or she wanted to.

TIP

In some states, such as California, the seller is prohibited from encumbering (adding additional financing) to the property above the amount due under the buyer's contract without first getting the buyer's permission. This applies even if the contract wasn't recorded.

2. The seller might take your money and then not make his or her own mortgage or tax payments. In other words, he or she just pockets the cash. Since it often takes months, sometimes years, for a lender to foreclose or a state to sell the property for back taxes, you might be making payments for a very long time before you learn what the seller is doing. And even when you learn, it could be very difficult for you to get your money back or to force a sale to you. In other words, you could lose everything you put into the property.

TIP

In many states the seller is required to first apply your (the buyer's) monthly install-ment payments to his or her mortgage and taxes. If taxes are not paid as part of the mortgage payment and are instead paid biannually, the seller must take the money you pay that's to go for taxes and hold it in a trust account until payment is due. (Many times, of course, the taxes are included with the monthly mortgage payment.)

3. You probably cannot get any financing based on your con-tract. Most lenders will not consider a contract for sale suf-ficient interest in the property to give you a loan based on it. Hence, you probably won't be able to get out any money you've paid in. And you won't be able to get a mortgage until you actually conclude the contract and get ownership.

4. You probably won't know for sure whether the seller actu-ally owns the property (has a good title to it) unless you have spent the money needed to obtain a title search or title insurance. (Indeed, you may not even be eligible for a policy of title insurance.)

TRAP

In a strange twist, some states have refused to let buyers out of the contract even though they later discover that the seller doesn't have a good title to the property. It's sort of an overly enthusiastic belief that "a contract is a contract."

5. You may not be able to transfer the contract to someone else. Remember, when we were discussing options in the last chapter, I mentioned that one clause you would want to be sure to have allows you to transfer your option to another party. Thus, if you couldn't exercise the option yourself and buy the property, you might be able to trans-fer it to someone who could and pocket a profit along the way. Unfortunately, many contracts for sale include a clause prohibiting or restricting transfers—for example, the contract may stipulate that an assignment or transfer may be made only with the seller's permission. Sellers

often insist on this as a way to ensure that they will know who is going to be making the payments.

6. After you go through the whole process, you might end up with a "defective" title. That might mean that the seller didn't own the property fully, that there were unknown liens against it (as, for example, might happen if creditors were after the seller), or there was some other "cloud" on the title.

How to Minimize the Risk. As with any purchase for which you do not get a clear title or title insurance to protect it, you can't eliminate the risks involved with contracts for sale. But you can try to minimize them.

- **Have the signatures on the contract notarized.** When they are notarized, the document can be recorded, and once recorded it gives notice that you have an interest in the property. This will make it more difficult for the seller to refinance or otherwise encumber the property. *Note*: You may be able to record a *memorandum of the land contract*. A memorandum usually just states what the contract says, and it is short, typically one page. It's less costly to record, but it still gives others notice that you have an interest in the property.

TIP

The seller may refuse to have his or her signature notarized. But you should be able to get yours notarized. Many states now allow the document to be recorded with only one party's signature notarized.

- **Pay for a title search yourself before you sign the contract.** A *condition of title report* may cost only a few hundred dollars, and it should reveal whether or not the seller actually owns the property and what debts he or she has placed on it. I would consider this step essential, even though it costs money out of your pocket. Any title insurance company can handle this for you.

- **Pay the taxes and insurance on the property yourself.** If you do this, you'll know they've been paid. Just have the agreement specify that you'll pay the taxes and insurance and have the amount deducted from your monthly payment. You may also be able to make payments on the seller's mortgage in a similar fashion. Keep in mind, however, that some sellers may balk at this, fearing that if you don't make the payments, they could lose the property. Often a compromise can be reached by having the party that pays send a copy of an acknowledgment of payment from the recipient to the other party.

- **Get a good attorney to draw up all the documents and advise you on how to minimize the risks even further in your locale.** Further, your state's laws may give you special protection, and your attorney should be able to spell this out for you.

How Do I Go About Getting a Contract for Sale?

Normally a contract for sale is handled between a buyer and seller. You need to find a seller who's willing to go along with you. How do you find such a seller? There are many ways similar to those we mentioned when looking for lease-option sellers.

- **Check newspaper ads.** Most sellers who are looking to give a contract for sale will advertise the fact. Often such contracts are offered for less expensive properties, so check out the ads at the lower end of the price range for your area.

- **Check the Internet.** Sellers often advertise on sites specifically aimed at buyers such as you. Use the keywords "land contract for sale."

- **Check housing offices.** You can check with local industries and larger employers, schools, churches, and any other places in your community that offer help in finding housing. Often you do not need to be a member of the organization to use the housing office. Sometimes notices will simply be posted on bulletin boards outside the offices.
- **Look for FSBO sellers.** You may be able to convert an FSBO into a seller who'll take a contract for sale. Just tour the neighborhoods you're interested in and look for "by owner" signs. Then approach the owner with your proposition. Keep in mind, however, that most owners want cash out of their property to put into their new home. The most likely contender to agree to a contract for sale is a seller who has a lot of equity.
- **Check around.** There are lots of sellers who would like to dispose of their property any way they can, but they aren't actively working at selling. This is especially true with rural properties. When you're looking at homes, look for vacant properties. An out-of-town owner might be willing to work with you on a contract for sale.

What about Real Estate Agents?

As with lease-options, the problem in obtaining the services of an agent is that he or she won't get a commission until you finally buy the home. Since that could be many years down the road, most agents are not going to want to work on this type of property transfer. In fact, that's the reason I say that most contracts for sale are handled directly between the buyers and sellers.

Nevertheless, there are an increasing number of agents around today who will work on a *fee-for-service basis*. In other words, they'll charge a flat fee for performing all the work required to do a contract for sale. If you can find such an agent in your area, typically the amount is only a thousand dollars or so. It might very well be worth the money to you.

Also, don't expect the agent to spend a lot of time looking for a seller willing to go along with a contract for sale. Again, there's unlikely to be a big commission involved—hence the lack of interest. You'll probably have to do all the scouting for this yourself.

Also see the section "Dealing with Agents" in Chapter 4.

Subject-To Purchases

This is a different technique for purchasing property that has been used more widely over the past few years. It allows buyers to purchase a home without obtaining new financing. In many cases it enables buyers to keep a low-interest-rate, low-payment mortgage that the seller already has on a particular property.

However, this technique, as we'll see, has some serious risks.

TRAP

Don't rush into a subject-to purchase without first consulting a good real estate agent and attorney who can explain the risks you face in your state. This is definitely a procedure that carries with it lots of challenges for the buyer.

A *subject-to purchase* means that you buy the property but you don't take over or pay off the seller's existing financing. Rather, the purchase is *subject-to* the financing. It remains in place with the seller's name on it. You're not obligated under it.

Think of it as if you were building a tower out of blocks. Part of the tower is already in place having been put there by the seller in the form of an old mortgage. You now add new blocks, in the form of new financing, onto the old blocks that are already in place making a taller tower.

An example should help. The seller wants $300,000 for her property that has an existing low-interest-rate, low-monthly-payment mortgage of $200,000 on it. You buy the property subject-to the existing mortgage—you don't touch it, assume it, or pay it off—and you agree to keep making the monthly payments on it. So instead of your obtaining entirely new financing, the seller gives you a new second mortgage for $100,000, and you put nothing down. The deal looks like this:

Subject-To Example

Existing mortgage	$200,000
New second mortgage	100,000 (from seller)
Purchase price	$300,000

Of course, the seller might just as easily give you a new $70,000 second mortgage, for which you would have to put 10 percent of the purchase price down, or $30,000.

Advantages of Subject-To Purchases

- You don't need to qualify for a new mortgage.
- The deal can be finalized with nothing-down or low-down financing; in fact, the seller often can handle any needed secondary financing.
- The monthly payments will be lower *if* the existing mortgage has a low interest rate.
- You're not obligated to make the payments on the existing mortgage.

A sweet deal, right?

But what's the catch?

The catch here is the lender. Lenders simply don't like the idea of a seller letting you buy the property *subject to* their existing mortgage. They want some say in the matter. They want to be able to raise the interest rate on the loan and to make sure you qualify for their mortgage. To do this, in short, they want to call in the mortgage and start over with a new (typically higher interest rate) mortgage for you, if you qualify. That's not something you probably want to do. If the lender calls in the existing mortgage, your tower can quickly fall to pieces.

How It All Started

Back in the 1950s buying a property on subject-to terms was simple. Lenders really didn't care who had the title to the property as long as the monthly payments kept rolling in. Whether it was the seller making the payments or you, the buyer, didn't really matter to the lender. Often all the buyer did was send a letter to the lender informing it of the subject-to sale, and the lender put the new owner's name on the mortgage. Clean and simple.

In the 1970s, however, a round of inflation hit, and mortgage rates went through the roof. Many existing loans had been written at 4 and 5 percent, but the new loans were going for 10 to 12 percent. Simply put, lenders (mostly savings and loans in those days) hated the idea of having low-interest loans on the books when there was money to be made on higher-interest loans. (If you were a lender, would you rather keep an old existing 5 percent mortgage or lend the same money out to a new borrower at 10 percent?)

Compounding this problem was the fact that lenders were being forced to pay higher interest to savings account clients. They were paying out 5 and 6 percent interest to savers, and their overhead typically was 2 percent. The total was far less than their old mortgages were bringing in at 4 and 5 percent. It was an untenable situation. And lenders became desperate. (Indeed, many were forced out of business.)

But while lenders wanted to call in those low-interest-rate mortgages, buyers and sellers saw this as an opportunity. Why pay off an existing 4 percent loan and replace it with a 9 percent loan when the buyer could simply purchase the home *subject-to* the loan? After all, virtually all of these were good, solid 30-year loans. A whole new way of selling real estate became popular, the subject-to way.

As a consequence of S&Ls going out of business because of the disparity between the old low-interest-rate loans that were kept on the books and new higher savings rates they were forced to pay, virtually *all* lenders began inserting a new *due-on-sale clause* (also called an *acceleration clause*) in every new mortgage they wrote.

TRAP

There's even a word for this, and it is *disintermediation*. In effect, it means that the mortgage lender, an intermediary between the seller and the buyer, is squeezed out. The seller deals directly with the buyer.

Due-on-Sale Clause

This is the seemingly innocuous clause that has been included in virtually every mortgage written in this country since the 1970s. It simply says that if the borrower-owner of the property sells the property (that is, the title changes hands), then the loan is *accelerated*, meaning that it immediately all comes due and payable. To enforce this, the lender can foreclose on the property, a process that can take anywhere from a few months to nearly a year, depending on the state in which you live.

Lenders wanted to be sure they weren't caught again in a squeeze where they couldn't call in lower-interest-rate loans when the market turned up a notch to higher interest rates.

It was good for the lenders. The consequences to sellers and buyers on subject-to purchases, however, were far reaching.

Now, as soon as the seller sold his or her property subject-to existing financing and the buyer *recorded* the deed, a transfer of the title took place. Because of the new clause, the lender was then well within its rights to accelerate the mortgage and insist that it be paid in full. This defeated the sellers' and buyers' gambit. It meant that the buyers couldn't buy properties without paying off the existing mortgages—no more subject-to purchases.

The due-on-sale clause was challenged in court in a variety of cases, and the most famous of them was *Wellenkamp vs. Bank of America* in California in 1978. Ultimately the California Supreme Court ruled against the lenders, saying that an institutional lender that was state chartered could not automatically enforce its due-on-sale clause simply because there was a title transfer. Rather, the lender had to show that the title transfer in some way impaired its security in the property.

This infuriated the lenders, and a flurry of new court cases ensued that dealt with the issue of federal law superseding state law, and it culminated in 1982 in the Garn-St. Germain Depository Institutions Act. It made the due-on-sale clause automatically enforceable for virtually all lenders. As of this writing and to the best of my knowledge, the due-on-sale clause is *completely enforceable.*

I'm sure some readers are wondering why this digression into a short history lesson. The reason it's important is because too much mistaken information on the due-on-sale clause has been disseminated by a few so-called real estate gurus including some book writers. They have pooh-poohed the clause, asserting that lenders either can't enforce it or don't really care about it since they never accelerate their mortgages anyhow.

As a result, some buyers have purchased property using a subject-to technique and have not taken into consideration the risks—what might happen if the lender accelerates (forecloses) on the mortgage. They've simply taken over making the seller's payments. They've adopted a "why worry" policy.

Since about 2005, however, interest rates have tended to rise. In a rising-interest-rate market, as noted earlier, it's to the lender's advantage to accelerate the mortgage when possible by using the due-on-sale clause.

TRAP

From about 2000 to 2005 mortgage interest rates tended to fall. During that time it is true that many mortgage lenders in fact did not enforce their due-on-sale clauses. It was simply economic pragmatism. Why should they accelerate a mortgage that was paying, for example, 8 percent when the best they could replace it with was a mortgage paying 5 percent? As long as the payments kept rolling in and interest rates were *falling*, many mortgage lenders turned a blind eye to their due-on-sale clauses. As a result, many buyers used the subject-to technique to successfully purchase property.

As a result, more recently we've begun seeing lenders once again enforcing their due-on-sale clauses to accelerate loans, particularly those that are well below the current market interest rate.

Does This Mean You Can't Make a Subject-To Purchase?

No, you can still buy a property subject to existing financing. It's just that you need to be aware of the possible consequences and be prepared to take appropriate action. For example, if you buy a property on subject-to terms and do not inform the lender of what you've done and the lender subsequently finds out and begins foreclosure, you need to be ready to refinance and pay off the existing lender with a new loan. If you don't successfully refinance or resell the property, you could lose it.

How Can the Lender Find Out?

I've listened to speakers say that mortgage lenders are just plain stupid. Unless you rub their noses in the information, they'll never know that the title has transferred. What they are saying is that unless you send a letter to a lender informing it of the title change, how would the lender ever find out?

These same speakers often point out that you want to be sure not to put a new return address on the checks or envelopes you send. I've heard some speakers even suggest carrying on this subterfuge by having the old owner continue to make the payment from his or her own checking account.

The fact of the matter is that almost always whenever a mortgage is recorded, right along with it is also recorded a Request for Notice of Transfer (or Alienation). This form goes by a wide variety of names depending on the state and locality. What it accomplishes is that whenever the title changes hands and that change is recorded, the recorder's office automatically sends a notice of that fact to the lender. Hence, the lender should know very soon after you buy the property if you've bought it on *subject-to terms* and recorded a new deed.

TRAP

Of course, there are mishaps. Sometimes the recorder's office fails to send the notice. Other times the notice is sent, but the address is incorrect (the lender has moved its offices). Other times the notice is sent and delivered, but it is lost, misplaced, or ignored by the lender. One lender with whom I spoke said that only about 50 percent of the time are the notices actually received and acted on by lenders.

Of course, the lender does not have to act and enforce the due-on-sale clause in the loan *if it doesn't want to*. It's at the lender's option. As we've seen, if interest rates are falling, a lender might simply choose to ignore the title transfer in order to keep receiving the monthly payments on a higher-interest-rate loan.

TRAP

Some attorneys with whom I've talked have discussed getting around the notification problem of the due-on-sale clause by sending a registered letter to the lender notifying it of the transfer in ownership. If, according to this tactic, the lender doesn't respond in a timely fashion (a few months), the presumption is that it has lost its right to accelerate the mortgage.

Maybe, but that tactic sounds pretty lame to me. The rule is quite clear that the lender has the right to exercise the due-on-sale clause on any transfer. Choosing when to exercise it would seem to likewise be in the lender's purview. I don't think you'd want to be involved in a court case to determine which position is correct.

What about Not Recording the Deed?

This argument centers on the belief that what the lender doesn't know won't hurt it. By not recording the deed transferring the title to you, you don't give constructive notice of the sale, and it's unlikely the lender will ever find out. If the lender doesn't find out, then you can keep the old low-interest-rate mortgage.

Maybe. The problem, of course, harkens back to the problems inherent with lease-options and contracts for sale. If you don't record a deed in your favor, it's possible the seller could put more mortgages on the property, lose it in a bankruptcy, or even resell it to someone else! Remember, recording the deed (and obtaining title insurance) is the best assurance you have that you actually own the property.

What about Notifying the Lender and Asking to Be Put on the Mortgage?

This is like an *assumption*. In a typical assumption, the seller's name is taken off the mortgage and the buyer's name replaces it. The buyer, so to speak, *assumes* the debt.

The trouble is that most loans today are not assumable. The due-on-sale clause precludes it, unless the mortgage specifically allows assumptions.

TIP

Some FHA and VA loans remain assumable. Also, many ARMs (adjustable-rate mortgages) are so-called assumable. However, in order to assume one of these mortgages, the buyer must qualify for the mortgage. In addition, usually the interest rate is bumped up to the market rate at the time. So it's the equivalent of getting a brand-new loan.

Another option is to notify the lender and ask that the buyer's name be *added* to the mortgage, without taking the seller's name off. In this case both the buyer and ultimately the seller remain responsible for the payback of the loan.

I understand that some lenders are willing to do this, particularly when the title transfer is to a family member. However, as a general rule, when interest rates are rising, you can probably expect a negative answer.

How Can You Use a Subject-To Gambit to Successfully Buy a Home?

Remember, the acceleration of the loan is at the option of the lender. If interest rates are falling, it's not to the lender's advantage to accelerate the mortgage. Why call in a performing loan at 8 percent when the best it might be replaced with is a loan at 7 percent? Why call in a loan paying at 6 percent when it would be replaced by one at 5 percent? As far as the lender is concerned, it may not care who owns the property—as long as payments are made. This certainly was the case for many subject-to buyers during the early 2000s.

Of course, once rates turn around, these very buyers could find the lender suddenly far more interested in the loan and suddenly calling it in under the due-on-sale clause. Thus, while the buyer might have a period of time, perhaps even several years, eventually the lender might act.

TRAP

Remember, it's a different story when interest rates are rising. Now a lender who has a loan performing at 5 percent can call it and perhaps replace it with a 6 or 7 percent loan. The incentive here is to accelerate the mortgage to get more interest.

What buyers who make subject-to purchases need to have is an escape plan. This means that in the event the lender exercises the due-on-sale clause, the buyer can refinance to a new mortgage and pay off the old one that's being accelerated. This, of course, assumes that appropriate new financing is available for which the buyer can qualify. Or it could involve selling the property assuming that the market is strong and selling at a good price is possible.

Remember, it usually takes time to accelerate the mortgage, and during that time, the new owner must secure the new financing or resell the property.

Nothing Down *and* Lower Monthly Payments

Perhaps I've convinced you to stop renting and buy a home. But you're strapped for cash—not only don't you have money for the down payment and closing costs, but you don't want to pay any more monthly than you're paying now. Heck, you don't even want to pay what your rent costs toward a mortgage because your rent's too high as it is!

Is there any way you can still buy a home without using the techniques outlined in the previous two chapters?

Very likely there is. It all depends on how well you can use (some would say manipulate) real estate financing to your advantage. In Chapter 3 we discussed mortgage tricks you can use. Here we're going to look at the details of how it's actually done. You just might be able to take advantage of some of these to get you into the home of your dreams without paying any more (possibly paying less!) than your current rent payments. And with little to no cash invested!

TIP

Get preapproved. The first step in financing a home is to get to a mortgage broker or direct lender and find out how big a monthly payment and mortgage amount you qualify for. By filling out a short application and getting a credit report and score, the mortgage broker-lender can quickly tell you. Once you know, you can start threading the path of different types of mortgages detailed below.

Solution 1: An ARM (but Not a Leg!) for Lower Payments

The traditional mortgage has a fixed interest rate. You get the mortgage, presumably for 30 years, at 5 or 8 percent or whatever, and you get a fixed monthly payment. The interest rate and the monthly payment are set in stone for the life of the loan—they never change.

The advantage of this mortgage is that you always know where you stand. At any given time, you'll know exactly how much you'll owe each month. (It's a great loan to get when interest rates are low.)

TRAP

For this chapter we're talking *only* about mortgages for which you actually move into the property—where you become an occupant owner. This is very important to remember. If you're buying the house as an investment to rent out, most of these mortgages will *not* be available to you. Lenders prefer occupant borrowers. They figure you'll take better care of the property and will fight harder to keep it if you get into financial difficulties.

The disadvantage is that in terms of mortgages, this usually offers the *highest* interest rate and monthly payment at any given time. In short, you might be able to do better.

One way to get a lower monthly payment is to get an ARM. This has nothing to do with body parts. ARM is an acronym for *adjustable-rate mortgage*. Here the interest rate charged can move up and down . . . and so too can the payments.

However, because of its adjustability, lenders prefer this type of loan. After all, if market interest rates go up, they can jack up the interest rate on your mortgage. In effect, they're sharing some of the burden of market uncertainties with you. (If you're still not sure what an *adjustable rate* means, think of your credit card—chances are good it has an adjustable interest rate.)

In most cases an ARM is not really as good a mortgage as a *fixed-rate mortgage*. After all, as noted, some of the risk of interest rate fluctuations has been transferred to you from the lender. Hence, all things being equal, most people would prefer a fixed rate.

Hence, in order to entice you to get an ARM, lenders will typically offer you a lower initial interest rate and lower monthly payment. In extreme cases the initial interest rate can be as little as half what is currently being charged for fixed-rate loans, and the monthly payment can also be half!

Teasers

Sound too good to be true?

Actually, it is. Typically the initial interest rate, with its corresponding monthly payment, is only an *introductory* offer, good for a limited time. It could be for as short a time as just a month or as long a time as five years. (I've rarely seen ARMs with an introductory rate good for more than five years.)

This introductory rate is designed to lure you into getting the loan. That's the reason it's unofficially called the "teaser rate." It teases you with its low interest and low monthly payment. But once you get into the loan, the rate goes up, sometimes to higher-than-market rate (as it tries to recoup the money lost due to the teaser).

The ARM is actually the lender's answer to fluctuations in interest rates. As noted, it puts some of the risk onto the back of the borrower—you.

TRAP

True teasers are typically only a percentage point or so below market. Sometimes, however, you'll see an introductory rate that's half the market rate. The danger, here, is that the interest being "lost" by this introductory rate is actually being added to the mortgage principal. See "Dangers of Negative Amortization," below.

But, and this is important, if you're clever and sometimes swift, you can use an ARM to your advantage. You can get one with the biggest teaser for the longest time, and then, just when the lender wants to jack up the interest rate, you can pay it off by refinancing to a new loan. In effect, you get the advantages of the ARM without the disadvantages. Here's how it works.

Look for an introductory rate that's long term. In recent years this has meant teasers that last three to five years. During that teaser period the loan is locked into a low interest rate, sometimes close to half the market rate.

But don't dawdle during that teaser period. Instead, be constantly looking for other mortgages to refinance into, especially as you get close to the end of the teaser period. If you're careful, and to some extent lucky, you could end up with very low payments. And if you refinance into another ARM with another long teaser, you could end up with low interest rates and low monthly payments again and repeat it over and over!

TRAP

Most recently in the subprime market (discussed below), the availability of financing has decreased. Borrowers with lower credit scores suddenly found that they could not find lenders willing to give them new mortgages to refinance. And they could not sell because of poor market conditions. Hence, they lost their properties to foreclosure. This is a real possibility if you get into a mortgage with a low teaser rate and can't get out before it resets to a higher interest rate and payment. It's something to seriously consider before getting a low-payment ARM.

Risks of Hopping Teasers

Nothing is risk free. And hopping between mortgages with teasers is no exception. Here are some of the problems you could face:

- **The loan has a prepayment penalty clause.** A *prepayment penalty* says that if you pay off your existing mortgage, typically before a certain amount of time has elapsed, you owe a penalty to the lender. Historically these penalties have been six months' worth of interest, a hefty sum. The lenders want these prepayment penalties in their mortgages so you can't easily jump from one ARM with a teaser to another. However, to be competitive and entice more borrowers, many lenders don't include them in their ARMs. Be sure to ask if the mortgage you are considering includes a prepayment penalty and what its conditions are. You might want to shop elsewhere to avoid it.

- **You can't qualify for a refinance.** Today you've got a solid job and you're making good money. You easily get the new mortgage with the teaser. Tomorrow, who knows? You could be out of work, and you might not be able to qualify for a refinancing. (You must qualify afresh each time you get a mortgage.) While this may seem to be only a remote possibility, it's a risk and something you should consider before deciding to mortgage hop.

- **The market changes and new ARMs with teasers aren't available.** ARMs have been around for about 30 years and so have teasers. But they haven't always been as generous as in recent years. In the future, low-interest-rate–low-monthly-payment teasers might not be available. This means that even if you refinanced, you might end up with higher interest rates and higher monthly payments—sometimes much higher. Again, it's a risk to consider.

I've known many buyers who have opted for an ARM with a big, long-term teaser. It's enabled them to get into a property they couldn't otherwise afford. And it's given them very low monthly payments. But, they've been aware of the risks. Don't even consider this option until you fully understand the consequences of being unable to refinance or resell when the loan resets to a higher interest rate and payment.

Note: There's more to an ARM than a teaser rate. There are indexes, margins, steps, and more, and all of these are important considerations. Check the Appendix for much more information on ARMs.

Solution 2: Interest-Only Mortgages

Yet another way to reduce the monthly payments is to pay only the interest on the mortgage.

It's important to understand that most mortgages provide for payment of interest and principal. That's how they are paid off. Each month a lot of the payment goes to pay the interest. And, at least initially, a small amount goes to pay the principal. (We saw the effect of this on equity return in Chapter 1.)

Again, think of the credit card example. There, in many cases you can choose to pay just the interest on the outstanding balance rolling it over each month.

For example, if you borrow $200,000 at 7 percent for 30 years and the loan is fully amortized, the first payment of $1,331 is broken down as follows.

Monthly Payment Breakdown

To interest	$1,167
To principal	164
Total monthly payment	$1,331

Here the monthly payment is $1,331. However, it could be reduced if you opted not to pay off the mortgage—that is, not to pay anything to the principal. In that case your monthly mortgage payment would be reduced by $164 down to $1,167.

What are the consequences of doing this?

Obviously, the biggest, and for many people the most important, consequence is a significantly lower monthly payment. By paying interest only, you've knocked your payment down by 14 percent (in our example). That's pretty significant if you're struggling to get the payment low enough so that you can buy a home.

Another big consequence, however, is that you're not paying off the mortgage. Were you to keep this mortgage for 30 years, at the end of that time, you'd still owe what you had originally borrowed: $200,000. On the other hand, were it a fully amortized loan, by the end of 30 years it would be completely paid off.

TIP

Remember, *amortized* means the loan is paid off a little bit each month until it's all paid back to the lender; *nonamortized* means it's not paid back—you're only covering the interest.

Of course, it's far nicer to have a paid-off home after 30 years than one with a big mortgage on it. On the other hand, here are some reasons why many borrowers do opt for the interest-only mortgage.

Reasons for Getting an Interest-Only Mortgage

- **Inflation.** Over 30 years the existence of inflation will very likely mean that the amount you originally borrowed will be worth far less in then current dollars. Consider what $200,000 borrowed 30 years ago is worth today in buying power—much less. That means you'll be paying back the mortgage 30 years from now in tomorrow's dollars.
- **You won't keep the mortgage for the full 30 years.** Most people sell their homes within around eight years. If you pay it off after eight years with or without amortization, you'll still have a significant payoff (remaining mortgage

amount). In our example, if the $200,000 were fully amortized, at year 8 you'd still owe $179,000. Over eight years you'd only have paid down roughly $21,000. (Most of the money goes to principal in the later, not the earlier, years of the mortgage). Maybe it's worth $21,000 to you eight years from now not to have bigger payments today?

Chances are that the value of your home will have appreciated during those intervening years, and you'll have much more money to play with at sales time. Of course, this is a risk as the value could go the other way. But historically, real estate has gone up in value.

How Do I Get an Interest-Only Mortgage?

Most lenders now offer these mortgages quite routinely. You simply tell your mortgage broker or direct lender you want an interest-only mortgage. You should be able to choose from a selection of mortgages and lenders.

TIP

Combine interest-only with an ARM. In this way you can get the best of both worlds and a much lower monthly payment. Just remember, however, that you also multiply the risks—you'll need to refinance a higher mortgage amount because nothing will have been paid down during your term of ownership.

Solution 3: 100 Percent Financing for Nothing Down

Let's suppose that instead of the monthly payment, your biggest concern is the down payment. You simply haven't saved up any money, and as a result, you have no cash to put down. You need 100 percent financing, or close to it. How do you go about getting it?

The answer could be easy . . . or not so easy depending on your income and your credit score.

Today lenders rely heavily on credit scoring. The main scoring company, the Fair Isaac Company (or FICO), will look at a credit report and then based on what it says and sometimes additional information give you a *credit score*. This is a numeric way of assessing your likelihood of paying back on time the mortgage you borrow.

The credit score typically ranges between a low of 350 and a high of 850. (The actual range is not disclosed.) The national average is a bit over 700, which is typically high enough to get 100 percent prime (the lowest, best mortgage) financing. Of course, the higher your score, sometimes additional perks accrue. For example, you might get a slightly lower interest rate, lower closing costs, or a higher *loan-to-value* (LTV) *ratio* loan.

On the other hand, the lower your score, particularly if it's lower than about 660, the more difficult it is to secure the best financing. You might have to get a *subprime mortgage*, which means that you'd have to pay a higher (sometimes significantly higher) interest rate or get a lower LTV loan. And there could be additional closing costs. This market basically collapsed in 2007. We'll deal more with lower credit scores and subprime financing in Chapter 7.

Assuming you've got a fairly good FICO score, then the size of the mortgage you can get will largely depend on your income. You must have enough income to pay the monthly payments plus all of your other monthly costs. You'll be told this magic maximum amount when you're preapproved.

Finally, you now tell your lender or mortgage broker that you need a 100 percent mortgage. You don't want and can't afford to put any money down.

Very likely your lender-mortgage broker will consider one of the many plans offered by Freddie Mac or Fannie Mae. These are the national secondary mortgage lenders who finance a substantial portion of all mortgages in the United States. As of this writing, they have many plans that offer 100 percent or near-100-percent financing.

One disadvantage of Freddie Mac or Fannie Mae financing, however, is that they have a maximum mortgage amount. This number changes each December, and as of January 1, 2007, it's $417,000. You can get financing up to 100 percent of the amount, but not more.

Jumbo (Elephantlike) Mortgages

Here we're talking *big*!

If you need a mortgage above the maximum limit for conforming loans, you are now looking at what the industry generally calls a *jumbo loan*. They are loans up to $650,000. Over that amount they're generally called *superjumbos*.

You are likely to need such a mortgage if you're living on the coasts where prices for real estate are much higher than elsewhere. Fortunately, in those areas such loans are readily available.

But there's a price to pay. Prime jumbos can require that the borrower have more assets than for a conforming loan and have a better credit score. On the other hand, it is still possible to get jumbo loans with close to nothing down.

The same people who offer you smaller-amount prime loans can direct you to jumbos. The procedure is essentially the same: You fill out an application, provide the required documentation, and get an appraisal. Then if everything checks out, you get approval and funding.

Often jumbos are in the form of two mortgages: a maximum conforming loan (Freddie Mac and Fannie Mae) and then a second loan that piggybacks on top of the first one. The interest rate on these piggyback loans is a blend of the conforming rate and the usually higher jumbo rate, which usually means a slightly lower combined interest rate and payment for you (that is, lower than a single jumbo loan).

A jumbo can be either a fixed rate or an ARM.

Solution 4: FHA and VA Government Insured or Guaranteed Mortgages

Yet another option may be to get a mortgage through the Federal Housing Administration (FHA) under the Department of Housing and Urban Development (HUD) or the Department of Veterans Affairs (formerly the Veterans Administration, the VA).

Contrary to popular belief, neither the FHA nor the VA normally makes loans directly to consumers. Rather, the FHA insures lenders against loss, and the VA guarantees the loans to lenders. Hence, the normal lenders, such as banks, are willing to make more favorable loans.

FHA Loans

Under the FHA program, you put as little as 3 percent down. The mortgage you get is assumable, providing that the buyer qualifies as to income and credit (but the next buyer gets to take over the existing interest rate). There are no prepayment penalties if you want to pay off the mortgage. And the property has to qualify, meaning that in some cases sellers are required to fix up substandard buildings.

With FHA loans, the maximum loan amount will vary depending on the area of the country and whether the property is rural or metropolitan. As of this writing, the maximum amount of the FHA mortgage in the continental United States is around $417,000. To find out the maximum FHA loan in your area as well as more information on FHA loans, go to the following Web site: www.hud.gov/buying/index.cfm.

VA Loans

To get a new VA loan, you must be a veteran and have qualifying duty. (See the Web site listed below to find out what terms are currently qualifying.) If you qualify, then you can get a no-down-payment mortgage. (There is a funding fee that is usually 2 percent of the mortgage amount or less, which may be incorporated into the loan.) Further, the VA requires many of the buyer's closing costs to be picked up by the seller. And the loan is assumable.

One of the unusual features of VA loans is that the veteran often remains on the hook for the loan if he or she allows someone else to later buy the property and assume the mortgage.

To get a VA loan, you must check with the VA and find out if you qualify. If you do, you'll be given an "entitlement," which will determine the amount you can borrow. When you later apply for a mortgage, the VA appraises the property and gives you a Certificate of Reasonable Value, which emphasizes the maximum you should pay.

The maximum VA loan as of this writing is generally the same as for conforming loans, which comes out to $417,000, although the VA uses its own formula to arrive at this amount. For more information on VA loans, check out this Web site: www. homeloans.va.gov/.

Sources for FHA and VA Loans

You can get both VA and FHA mortgages from mortgage brokers and direct lenders such as banks. They are fairly common in the midsection of the country, but because of their low maximum loan amounts, they are used less often on the coasts.

TRAP

Because the terms of VA and FHA loans are frequently in flux, it's important to check them out well in advance of attempting to secure one.

Solution 5: 100 Percent Seller Financing

Perhaps the best type of no-down-payment financing comes directly from the seller. Here the seller carries back *paper* (a mortgage) for the price of the property. You buy the home, and the seller gives you a mortgage for the full purchase price. What could be simpler?

The problem is that in order for a seller to completely finance your purchase, the seller must either own the property free and clear or be able to pay off any small existing mortgage. About 25 to 30 percent of the properties in the country qualify, so you do have some choices here but obviously not as many as you would have if you had a new mortgage from a lender.

The other option is for you to have a new 80 percent mortgage from an institutional lender (thus paying off the seller's old financing) and then have the seller carry back a small 20 percent second mortgage on the property. Here the seller needs to have only at least 20 percent equity in the home to make the deal work. Of course, first you need to qualify for the institutional mortgage.

TRAP

It is possible to buy a home from the seller subject to an existing mortgage—that is, not assume or pay off the seller's existing loan. However, it is fraught with perils. Check Chapter 5 for more details.

When outside lenders won't give you a nothing-down mortgage (because of your credit problems or the unavailability of such financing), combining an institutional first with a seller's second can work well to get into a property with nothing down. Of course, you have to find an agreeable seller.

How Do You Get a Seller to Finance Your Purchase?

As we've seen with real estate financing, when a seller carries back paper, he or she is creating a mortgage with the buyer as the borrower. The buyer, in essence, is loaned a portion of the seller's equity in order to be able to purchase the home.

To find out if a seller will go along with this, you must ask. You would ask usually in the form of an offer to purchase in which the purchase agreement includes a financing contingency calling for the seller to carry back paper. Any good real estate agent can prepare this for you including specifying the exact terms of the new loan.

You can make this offer to any seller. However, usually it works best if the seller has previously indicated a willingness to carry back paper. (And, of course, the seller must have sufficient equity.) Also, when market conditions favor buyers over sellers and it's hard to move a property, sellers are more inclined to look with favor on financing their property.

TRAP

Sometimes outside lenders frown on second mortgages. Some lenders are applying a *combined loan-to-value* (CLTV) ratio to their first mortgages. This is a combined first and second loan-to-value ratio. What this means is that *all* loans on the property cannot exceed a certain percentage. For example, a lender might have a 90 percent CLTV, meaning that if you got a 20 percent second from the seller, the lender would lend you only 70 percent, making you still 10 percent shy of nothing down. If you need to work with a seller's second mortgage, be sure the lender of the first does not use CLTV ratios.

Check the Terms Carefully

Since you're creating the mortgage with the seller, you can craft the terms to fit your needs. Of course, the sellers are probably working hard to do the same thing to their advantage. Therefore, be sure to check the terms closely. Look for the following:

- **A lower interest rate.** The interest rate with the seller is completely negotiable, and it will usually determine the size of the monthly payment. You may be able to get a lower-than-market rate from a desperate seller.
- **A longer term.** A second can be for any length of time. It can be for 3 months or 3 years or 30 years. It's all up to what you and the seller agree on. In most cases the longer the term, the

better for you, the borrower. Most sellers want seconds for a relatively short time, 18 months to 5 years, in order to get their money out as quickly as possible. Often during that time you pay interest only, which means at the end, you still owe the full amount that you borrowed—a balloon payment. As a result, you must usually refinance or sell the home before the term of the seller's financing runs out. Naturally, the longer the second, therefore, the better it is for you.

TRAP

Beware of very short-term seconds. You can never know what the market will be like even just a few months into the future. Your risk increases the shorter the term. The more years you have on your second, usually the better for you.

Automatic Renewals

An important clause to have in a second is an automatic renewal. This allows you to roll the second mortgage over when it comes due. You want this at *your* option, not the seller's.

With an automatic renewal, when the second comes due, if you can't refinance or resell, you simply roll the second over for a second term. Many sellers will go along with a one-time automatic renewal. Offering to increase the interest rate at renewal time is usually a good incentive to get sellers to go along.

Seller financing offers all kinds of opportunities to get into a property with nothing down. It's really limited only by your imagination and what you and the seller can agree on.

Solution 6: Reducing Your Payments by Eliminating the PMI

One of the things we haven't really discussed is *private mortgage insurance* (PMI). Any time you get a mortgage from an institutional lender (such as a bank) and that loan is for more than an 80 percent LTV ratio, the lender is required to carry PMI. This *insures the lender* against loss should you fail to make your payments and foreclosure becomes necessary.

Unfortunately, the cost of the PMI is paid by you, and it is added to your monthly payment. The amount is based on risk. Thus, the PMI will be higher for a 95 percent loan than for a 90 percent loan. And higher still for a 100 percent loan.

The charge also will depend on the amount of the loan that's insured. The lender can choose to insure the top 18 percent or the top 37 percent of the mortgage. The more of the mortgage covered, the higher the cost. (*Top* means the coverage is from the maximum amount downward. For example, 18 percent coverage on a $200,000 loan means that the insurer would pay to the lender the first $36,000 of the mortgage should you default and foreclosure becomes necessary.)

How much does that insurance translate into additional cost for you? It varies, but it can be quite high. Usually the low is a quarter of 1 percent while the high can be three-quarters of 1 percent or more. On a $300,000 mortgage, 3/4 percent is $2,250 spread over 12 months, meaning that you're paying almost $200 a month (actually $187.50) just for PMI costs. To most borrowers, that's a hefty sum. If you could avoid the PMI, you could reduce your payments (in this case) by almost $200.

Getting Rid of the PMI

One way to reduce your monthly payments is to get rid of the PMI portion. Though lenders seldom point it out, at a certain point several years into the loan, you may be able to get the PMI removed from your loan.

TRAP

Sometimes the PMI fee is written into the mortgage as part of the interest rate. If so, you can never get it removed. You can get the PMI removed *only* if it's charged as a separate PMI fee.

The federal Homeowners Protection Act of 1998 dealt with the issue of removing the PMI. Basically it mandates that the PMI automatically be canceled whenever the balance of your loan drops to 78 percent of the value of the property at the time the loan was made. In other words, if you bought a $200,000 property with a 90 percent loan ($180,000), that mortgage would have to drop to $156,000 for the PMI to automatically cancel out. In terms of actual time, that's something like seven to nine years after you get the mortgage.

Of course, that doesn't take into account price appreciation. The same federal Homeowners Protection Act provides a procedure for petitioning the lender to have the PMI removed earlier. This applies *if:* Your equity equals at least 20 percent of the current value of the property (25 percent if it's a Fannie Mae or Freddie Mac mortgage); you pay for an appraisal by an appraiser designated by your lender and if that appraisal verifies your equity (if the appraisal comes in low, the lender doesn't have to remove the PMI and you're out the cost of the appraisal); and if you can show a history of on-time payments for the last year. Further, at least two years must have elapsed since you obtained the mortgage.

It would be a mistake to expect a lender to come to you with a suggestion for removing the PMI no matter how much your house appreciates or how much of the mortgage you pay down. They have no incentive to do so, and at best, it just means extra accounting for them. That means that you must get the ball rolling yourself.

A Way to Get around PMI When You Buy

In the above discussion, we saw how to get PMI removed once you've acquired the home and mortgage (after waiting a few years). However, that doesn't help very much when you want to make a purchase. Is there any way to avoid PMI when you're buying?

As a matter of fact, there is, and we've already discussed it. Remember, PMI is required only when the mortgage is for more than 80 percent of the purchase price (that is, it's an 80 percent LTV ratio mortgage). If you get an 80 percent mortgage or less, you aren't required to make the extra PMI payment.

So get an 80 percent mortgage, and have another lender (or the same one) or the seller carry back a 20 percent second. If there's a 20 percent LTV second, no PMI is required on either loan. And you can save a substantial amount of money.

TIP

If you get the seller to carry back the second, be sure to also negotiate a lower-than-market interest rate—something that's possible in a slow market. That way not only do you save on PMI charges but you also get an even lower payment because of the lower interest rate on 20 percent of your financing.

Solution 7: Absolutely Minimum Payments with the Option Mortgage

Thus far we've looked at most of the options available to you when you want to get the lowest payment possible. However, there's one that we've not yet touched on, and it's called the *option mortgage*.

The option mortgage offers you the opportunity to get the very lowest monthly payment—zero! That's right, with some option mortgages you can opt to simply not make a monthly payment. Is that low enough?!

Of course, as with most things that seem too good to be true, this is just that. The option mortgage requires stiff discipline to manage, and it is filled with opportunities to do yourself harm. Many borrowers came to disaster in 2007 when option mortgages reset to higher interest rates and payments and they couldn't refinance or sell. This is an option, but not a panacea.

How Do Option Mortgages Work?

The option mortgage is the brainchild of mortgage lenders who were looking for a way to hook borrowers at a time near the end of the last real estate boom when they had a lot of money to lend and not very many people looking to get it. This mortgage depends on a lot of different banking rules that when blended together, form a kind of Frankenstein's monster of finance.

This is not to say that there's anything innately wrong with the option mortgage. It's simply a tool that like any other tool can be used to benefit . . . or to harm.

Basically, the option mortgage is exactly what it says it is. It gives you, the borrower, the option (the right) to decide how you want to handle your monthly payment each month. When you obtain the mortgage, a variety of monthly payment options are given to you. These will vary depending on the lender and the mortgage program. Here are some typical options.

Typical Option Mortgage Choices for Making the Monthly Payment

- **Make your regular monthly payment.** Often you have an ARM, and the interest is calculated monthly; thus your monthly payment will vary a lot depending on the current market interest rate. Some option mortgages feature a fixed-rate mortgage, and in that case, the basic monthly payment is also fixed. Here part of your payment goes to principal and part to interest.
- **Choose to pay interest only.** In any given month, you can decide not to pay anything toward principal. Rather, you pay only the interest due at the current time. Since interest on mortgages is always paid in arrears (as opposed to rent, which is paid in advance), the exact amount can easily be

calculated regardless of whether your mortgage is a fixed-rate mortgage or an ARM.

- **Choose to pay a reduced payment.** As stipulated by the mortgage documents, the reduced payment could be, for example, 50 percent of your regular monthly payment. Any interest not paid would be added to your mortgage. (See "Dangers of Negative Amortization" below.) This is designed for times when your other bills are unusually heavy and you need a month or so to catch up.

- **Choose to skip a payment; pay zero.** As above, this is designed for emergencies, as when you're between jobs or need funds to cover a medical crisis. The interest not paid, as above, is added to your mortgage.

- **Designate a portion of your payment to go to life and/or mortgage insurance.** This feature is found primarily on mortgages offered through mortgage brokers by insurance companies. Again, any interest not covered because you've designated a portion of the payment to go to insurance is added to the mortgage. (Beware of lenders slipping this into the mortgage at the closing, when you may not be paying close attention!)

- **Pay a higher monthly payment.** At any time you can pay more than the minimum amount and designate it to go to principal, thus more quickly paying off your mortgage.

- **Any other option put in by the lender and agreed upon by you.** Obviously this is a very creative mortgage. There can be all sorts of other options included by the lender.

Thus, each month you can choose to make your payment based on any of the options. For example, one month you could make a full, basic payment. The next month you could skip the payment and have the interest added to the mortgage amount. The third month you could pay only the interest alone for that month. And so on.

Advantages of Option Mortgages

The big advantage, of course, is that you can control your monthly payment. You can adjust it to fit your financial situation. Ideally when times are good for you, you can pay a higher monthly payment. When times are rough, you can pay less, or even nothing. Thus, the option mortgage gives you far greater control over financial destiny.

Of course, it also lets you get into a property with the lowest possible monthly payment.

Dangers of Option Mortgages

One great danger of the option mortgage is the temptation to pay interest only, a reduced payment, or no payment every month. We all have many bills, and usually we're spread very thin. When we look at all the bills we have to pay and realize that this month we can pay interest only, or reduced interest, or even skip a payment, we can't help but be tempted.

If we only do this once in a while, the consequences will probably be very slight. However, the temptation arises every month, and pretty soon we could find ourselves adding interest to interest every month on our mortgage. Instead of being paid off, the amount of money we owe could grow, and that could eventually overwhelm us.

TRAP

It takes iron discipline to force oneself to make the full monthly payment on a regular basis. That's why this loan should be used only by borrowers who have the willpower to resist the temptation of making reduced payments on a regular basis.

Dangers of Reduced Monthly Payments

The other great danger of the option loan is that it's usually for a relatively short time—typically one to five years. It is only during that time that you can exercise your option.

At the end of that time, the mortgage *resets*. That means that the new principal amount (remember all that interest added on?) is now amortized over 30 years as an ARM at the market interest rate. When this happens, you could see your payment jump dangerously high. (Many option loan borrowers in 2007 saw their monthly payments double!) In order to avoid such high payments, you would have to refinance or resell, and we've seen that these options are not always possible.

Dangers of Negative Amortization

Possibly the worst concept ever introduced in mortgage banking goes by the rather innocuous name of *negative amortization*. In Chapter 1 we discussed how amortization—that is, the regular repayment of a mortgage—leads to equity return, which has always been one of the big plusses offered by homeownership.

This is the exact opposite. Instead of owing less each month, you end up owing more. Every time you pay less than the monthly interest on your mortgage, the amount of interest not paid is added to the outstanding balance. Thus your mortgage grows bigger and bigger, not smaller.

Further, you now begin paying interest not only on the principal that you originally borrowed but also on the interest previously added to that principal. In short, you end up paying interest on interest.

This is such an unethical method of financing that there are even Biblical prohibitions against it. (Paying interest on interest used to be the exclusive purview of the Mob!) Yet as long as you agree, it's not illegal in American banking. Generally speaking, the banking laws allow the amount of your mortgage to grow up to 125 percent of its original amount by having interest added to the principal.

TRAP

Be sure you understand exactly what you're getting. Too often in their haste to get into a property, borrowers neglect to ask about the perils of negative amortization. And some lenders have not always been fully up front about explaining it. Ask if your mortgage negatively amortizes. Ask for examples of how this works. Be sure you understand and agree to it before moving forward on your mortgage.

The theory behind allowing negative amortization is that since property prices are moving upward, the borrower won't get hurt. Eventually you'll sell the property for more than you paid, so what's the harm in a higher mortgage? Put another way, it's a method by which the lender can share in the appreciation of your property. Of course, when times change and prices are stagnant or even move down, it's a different story.

TIP

I've had discussions with bankers on the point of negative amortization who see no moral issue involved and no ethical problem. Rather, they see it as a positive solution to getting a lower monthly payment. Many borrowers feel exactly the same way.

Of course, if you opt for a lower monthly payment with negative amortization and it happens to be at a time when real estate prices are stagnant, or worse, falling, it could mean you'll become *upside down*. That means that you could owe more than the property's worth. This makes it almost impossible to sell or refinance.

My suggestion is to avoid negative amortization whenever possible. To my mind, it's just not sound economics or financing.

Solution 8: Getting around the Closing Costs

Finally, there are the transaction costs involved in any real estate purchase. The total costs for a *round-trip*—buying and then reselling—average around 10 percent or more. That includes the commission when you sell and escrow and title insurance costs when you buy and sell.

For the buyer alone, the costs are typically under 4 percent. Those include the following expenses.

Typical Buyer's Closing Costs

- **Points charged by the lender.** Each point is equal to 1 percent of the loan amount. For example, if the lender requires 3 points and the mortgage is $200,000, that's $6,000. Sometimes points can be tax deductible—check with your accountant.
- **Fees charged by the lender.** These expenses can be minor, major, or excessive. When excessive, they are frequently called *garbage fees*. You should shop around for lenders who offer the lowest and fewest fees.
- **Title insurance.** This fee is sometimes paid by the seller, sometimes split between seller and buyer, and sometimes paid by the buyer. It all depends on what's commonly done in your area. The fee is sometimes set by the state, but most often it is determined by the title insurance company. You should shop around to find the best title insurance fees.
- **Escrow charges.** These expenses are typically split between buyer and seller. The fees vary enormously; thus it pays to shop for a cheaper escrow company *before* you open escrow.

All of the above fees to the buyer can amount to many thousands of dollars. In some cases they can amount to 5 percent or more of the purchase price, so they're not cheap. And they can be a real problem if you're trying to buy a property with little or no cash in your wallet.

TIP

Points trading has become fairly common among borrowers and lenders. Here points are traded against the interest rate. If you want fewer points, you can get them by paying a slightly higher interest rate and higher monthly payments. If you have cash, you can pay more points and get your interest rate and monthly payments reduced. Ask your lender.

Have the Lender Absorb Your Closing Costs

Today, if you have a good credit score, you can have the lender absorb most if not all of your closing costs. It's done in one of two ways.

The first way is to add the closing costs to your mortgage balance. For example, you have a $100,000 mortgage and your closing costs are $3,000. They are added to the mortgage bringing the balance to $103,000. Lenders in most cases can easily increase the mortgage amount to 103 percent of the LTV ratio. In some cases it can be increased to 107 percent—talk to your lender.

The second method involves the interest rate. The lender absorbs the closing costs, and you end up with a slightly higher interest rate. Depending on the amount of the closing costs, the interest rate increase is typically between $1/4$ and $1/2$ percent. For example, your market interest rate might be 6 percent. But you have the lender pay your closing costs, and you end up with an effective rate of 6 $3/8$ percent (the $3/8$ percent is added to cover your closing costs).

TRAP

Whether the lender increases the mortgage amount or increases the interest rate, you'll end up with a slightly higher monthly payment. Remember, nothing in life is free.

Ask your mortgage broker or direct lender about folding the closing costs into the mortgage by either of the above two methods. If you get stonewalled and are told it can't be done, look elsewhere. It's being done all over the country all the time.

Having the Seller Pay Your Closing Costs

This is a negotiating ploy. When you're bargaining over the purchase of the home, you make one of the conditions of purchase
that the seller must pay your closing costs. Put simply, you say you
won't buy unless the seller does this.

Will sellers actually pay your closing costs?

Sellers do it all the time. Whether yours will or not really
depends on the market at the time and the individual seller. When
the market is slow and sellers are having trouble moving property,
they are much more likely to be agreeable. After all, it's either pay
your costs or there's no sale.

On the other hand, when the market is booming, houses are
selling quickly, and buyers are waiting in line, sellers are much
more reluctant to pay a buyer's costs. They figure if you don't buy
it today, there'll be two others who want to buy it tomorrow.

Also, the individual seller makes a big difference. Some sellers
are practical, and to make a sale they will go along. Others find it
objectionable to pay the other party's costs on principle, and they
will simply refuse out of hand.

The only way you can find out is to ask, in the form of incorpo-
rating the request as a contingency clause in your purchase agreement—something any good real estate agent can insert.

TRAP

When you're negotiating in real estate, if you insist on one thing, you might have
to give up something else. For example, if you insist on the seller paying your closing costs, the seller might insist on a slightly higher price. It's tit for tat, and such
compromise is not unreasonable. Don't expect to get it all—lower price, seller
financing, seller paying for closing costs, and so on—unless the market is very
slow, the seller is desperate, or the house is a wreck.

Note: Many lenders will not allow the seller to pay your *recurring closing costs*—that is, such things as mortgage interest in the
form of points, taxes, and so on. They figure that if you can't

afford to handle these yourself, you probably can't afford to make the purchase.

On the other hand, few lenders will object to the seller paying your *nonrecurring closing costs*—such as title insurance, escrow charges, and some loan fees that only occur once.

By having either the lender or the seller absorb your closing costs, it should be possible for you to find a house that you can get into for virtually nothing down *and* almost no closing costs.

For more information on advanced financing techniques for your real estate purchase, check my book *Tips and Traps When Mortgage Hunting* (McGraw-Hill, 2005).

Getting Financing Even When Credit Is a Problem

We've discussed a wide variety of financing options for buying a home. However, most of them depend on your having good credit. That means your having a good credit score.

But what exactly is a "credit score"? And if you don't have a good one, can you improve a bad one?

What Can Hurt a Borrower's Credit?

Good credit can mean that you can finance a home purchase, and needless to say, bad credit can mean you may not be able to do it easily. But what causes a bad credit score?

Here's a list of factors that can cause your credit to deteriorate. Some of them may surprise you.

Causes of a Bad Credit Score

- **Too many applications for credit.** If you keep applying for new loans, it can drive your credit score down. Lenders wonder why you need all that credit. More than three applications in six months can be a problem.
- **Too high balances in your credit lines.** If all your *credit lines*—that is, your credit cards, car loans, personal loans, and so on—are maxed out, it suggests you have difficulty in managing credit. Keeping outstanding debt at less than 50 percent of your maximum available credit should help.
- **Not enough long-term credit lines.** Lenders love to see that you've had a credit card with a particular bank for a great many years. It suggests stability and a penchant to repay money lent to you. If you have three credit cards all just a few months old, it suggests you're just getting started and are an uncertain financial commodity.
- **Late payments.** Lenders love to see credit report comments such as "Never late" and "Always on time." Late payments suggest you either can't manage your finances or you don't have sufficient income to cover your debts.
- **Bad debts.** Here the credit report says that you ignored a debt and failed to pay it back. You could be in collection, and/or there could be a judgment against you. Why would a new lender want to give you a new mortgage when you haven't paid back a former lender?
- **Foreclosure.** Mortgage lenders hate this more than anything else. It says you didn't pay back money you borrowed on a house. See above and double that negative reaction. Foreclosures sometimes come off your credit report after a number of years, but in some cases they remain almost indefinitely.

- **Bankruptcy.** Seeing a bankruptcy on the report tells lenders that you attempted to discharge your debt through a bankruptcy proceeding. You may still owe money. In any event, a bankruptcy does not inspire a lender's confidence. Bankruptcies typically stay on your records for five to seven years.

TRAP

Some people are surprised to learn how much even a few late payments can affect their credit. When late payments show up on your credit report, it very quickly shoots down your credit score. The smart thing to do is to *always* make your payments on time. Some savvy consumers will even pay disputed bills immediately, then seek redress in small claims court, all to protect their credit standing.

When you have bad credit, you'll get a low credit score. And the lower your credit score, the less likely you'll be to be able to get good real estate financing.

What Is a Credit Score?

We've been talking about this quite a bit, but let's be sure we fully understand what it is.

A *credit score* is a numerical assessment of your credit status. It helps a lender determine how much of a risk you are. It suggests whether or not you'll pay your mortgage payments promptly.

When you apply for a mortgage, the lender gets a credit report. But a credit report is only figures on a piece of paper. How does the lender evaluate it? How does the lender translate that credit report into a risk assessment?

The answer is that lenders rely, in part, on special companies to do that evaluation for them. The most widely used of these credit scorers is the Fair Isaac Corporation (FICO) in California. The FICO company analyses your credit report and then gives you a score between 350 and 850. The higher your score, the better a credit risk you are. The lower your score, the more likely you'll be late on payments or default on your loan. (The average national FICO score is a bit over 700.)

TIP

If you've applied for a mortgage recently, chances are you have a FICO score, and you can learn what it is. Simply go to www.fairisaac.com online. (You can also obtain it through www.experian.com.) For $12.95 (current price) you'll get your score. The FICO site also provides all sorts of information on how your FICO score is determined and gives a few clues on how to raise it.

While each lender looks at the numbers differently, generally speaking if you have a score over 680, you're probably going to be able to get a good mortgage—one at the best interest rate and possibly with nothing down. Of course, a score over 800 will almost guarantee that outcome while a score *under* 600 may mean you'll need to look at a subprime loan (explained below).

How Does a Borrower Get a Credit Score?

When you apply for a mortgage, you'll be asked to fill out a standard loan application. It has about 60 questions on it, and it identifies whole categories of your personal finances including the following:

- Your expenses
- The amount of cash you're putting down
- Your gross household income
- Your cash on hand
- Your short- and long-term debt

And the lender will also ask your permission to get a credit report. (You might be asked to pay for this, typically under $50, but you should get the amount refunded if you eventually move forward and get the mortgage.) When the credit report comes back, the lender will also automatically secure a credit score. (With a three-bureau credit report, explained below, there may actually be three separate credit scores.) Interestingly, the lender will not immediately pass along the credit report(s) and score(s), although you can request copies that may be sent to you later. The lender, however, will be sending you a letter typically notifying you of your credit score and their reasons for denying you a mortgage, if they do so.

The lender will look at your income, your debt, and your credit score(s), and then using computerized financial profiling, the lender will attempt to determine the maximum monthly payment and loan amount you can afford.

TIP

There are three national credit bureaus: Experian, TransUnion, and Equifax. They receive and accumulate input from many other smaller credit reporting agencies around the country. Typically the lender will run a three-bureau credit check (also sometimes called a *standard factual*) that checks your credit as it is listed with all three companies, and it will get three different credit scores from these different companies as well. It will then take either the average of the three scores or, in some cases, the lowest of the three scores to use in your evaluation.

How Does a Lender Evaluate a Credit Score?

In today's real estate mortgage market, the company whose name appears on your monthly mortgage documents is probably only the *mortgage servicer*. It originates the loan and then packages and sells it, collecting payments from you.

However, the money itself ultimately often comes from one of two sources: Fannie Mae or Freddie Mac (called *secondary lenders*). These are huge quasi-government corporations that loan billions on real estate. Their underwriting departments are the ones who evaluate your credit score and other financial information.

The underwriters look at your application and your credit score(s) and then apply a financial profile. Depending on the results, they then approve or disapprove of the mortgage you want as well as indicate what they think you can afford.

What Is a Financial Profile?

Although most lenders never use that term because of its bad connotation, a *financial profile* is an important part of the loan-application-approval process. Underwriters use a database of millions of successful and not-so-successful borrowers. From this they create profiles of what successful mortgage applicants will look like. Then they try to fit you into one of these profiles.

It's important to understand that the development of modern profiling methods has meant that people who previously would never have qualified for a mortgage are now able to get one. Putting a larger down payment into a property may outweigh not having a big income. Having a good credit score and high income may mean being able to buy with nothing down. And so on. The evaluation of an applicant's financial profile depends on what people with similar financial profiles have done in the past.

What If a Borrower Has a Poor Financial Profile?

If you're a prime borrower, one with a terrific profile, the best loans are available to you. However, if you're a subprime borrower, other types of financing may still be available to you. There are many lenders out there who will offer financing to subprime borrowers. They'll just charge a higher interest rate (meaning higher monthly payments) and perhaps more points.

All of which is to suggest why keeping good credit remains your best insurance for getting great financing.

TRAP

Defaults by subprime borrowers over the last few years have curtailed many of the programs that catered to them. Today there are far fewer subprime lenders that tend to be far more choosy about whom they'll lend to.

How Can a Borrower Improve a Credit Score?

Most scoring companies suggest that it's possible to improve your score over time. The FICO company has pointed out that applying for credit too many times (more than three, for example) within a three- to six-month period could lower your score. Thus, by not submitting a lot of loan applications, you may be able to help your score, or at least not drag it down.

TIP

Checking out your credit by buying a credit report directly from a credit bureau is not supposed to count as applying for credit. So it's probably a good idea to check your credit before applying for a mortgage. That way you have time to correct any errors. (Some have suggested that errors crop up in credit reports as much as a third of the time.)

Improve Your Income

Try to show as much income as possible. Include alimony. If two spouses work, be sure to show both incomes. If they have had long careers, indicate that as well.

When filling out a mortgage application, it pays to emphasize length and continuity. Don't simply say you got your first job a year ago. Point out that you previously worked for 10 years, then left to raise a family, and are now just returning to the workforce. If you're in a career, medicine, for example, emphasize your career status.

Adjust Your Down Payment

If you have a credit problem, see if you can put more money down. Even going from 100 percent financing to 95 percent financing can help. The reason is the more you put into the property, the less likely, lenders feel, you are to let it go to foreclosure. If hard times hit, the more you have in it, presumably, the harder you'll fight to keep the home.

Of course, this applies only if you have the resources to put more money down. However, you may have more resources than you first imagine.

While borrowing the down payment can be a problem, getting a gift usually helps. Borrowing the down payment suggests to the underwriter that you really can't afford the property. On the other hand, gifts for the down payment are usually acceptable. These must, however, be legitimate gifts. They can't be given with strings attached, such as you'll repay them so much a month and when you sell the property you'll repay the balance in full. In that case, they are nothing more than a disguised loan.

If you need to borrow money that you intend to use for the down payment, borrow it at least six months before applying for the mortgage. That way you can put the money into a savings account, and it will be seen as a cash reserve. On the other hand, the loan for that money will likely be seen as part of long-term debt. Just remember, the more debt you have, the less of a mortgage you're likely to be able to get.

Have Proof of Your Income If You Are Self-Employed

If you're self-employed, you may have difficulty in getting a home loan. Sometimes prime loans simply will not be granted to self-employed individuals. In other cases your application will be considered if you can produce the last two years of your 1040 federal tax filings.

The concern is verifying your income—you could submit false records. (Today many lenders are capable of verifying income directly with the IRS!) And when you are self-employed, unless you can show a long work history, you are presumed to be at risk of job loss.

If you can show income as an employee, you're usually far better off when getting financing than if you can show income only as a self-employed person.

The best course of action for self-employed people would be to work with a mortgage broker in their area.

Establish Cash Reserves for Yourself

You need to have money left in the bank after you make the down payment and take care of the closing costs. Lenders usually would like to see at least three months' worth of cash on hand. If you have only a month or two, you could be turned down, or more likely, you may be asked to accept a smaller mortgage.

You can usually improve your credit standing by keeping a couple of months of cash in the bank.

Catch Up on Any Bad Debts

Lenders report bad debts or late payments to credit checking companies. Those credit checking companies also regularly scan public records to see if you have had any bankruptcies or foreclosures.

If you're behind in payments to any lender, be sure to catch up before applying for the mortgage. Try to stay caught up for at least a year before applying so your delinquencies will show up as old rather than recent. Old delinquencies are much easier to forgive.

TRAP

Repeated delinquencies can be a problem, even if you're caught up now. Try to always pay on time.

TIP

If you can't make the payments, don't borrow the money.

Bankruptcies are a big problem. However, if it's been more than two years, during which you maintained perfect credit, the bankruptcy may simply be ignored by the lender. A foreclosure listed on your credit, however, is almost never ignored. Lenders don't like to offer mortgages to people who have in the past lost their home to mortgage foreclosure.

But always check with a mortgage broker, and ask him or her to look into the possibilities of your obtaining a loan. Every situation is unique, and mortgage brokers sometimes know of options that conventional lenders are not aware of.

Other Things to Do

Here are some constructive tips for improving your credit score:

- Don't apply for credit for six months before you apply for a mortgage.
- Keep your credit cards well under their limits. Don't go over the limits even if your credit card lender agrees to extend them.
- Don't throw away your old credit cards. Instead, keep them active. You don't have to borrow on them. Just having old lines of credit is helpful.
- Have a mix of credit. You don't want a lot of loans, but having a car loan, three credit cards, and a department store card suggests you're a good credit manager. That's what the underwriters are looking for.

How Can a Borrower Fix Bad Credit?

Companies that offer to fix or make *any* credit problem simply disappear, particularly if they charge you a hefty fee for doing it, may be nothing more than con artists. On the other hand, today there are *credit fixers* out there who can do for you (for a fee) what you can do for yourself. Credit problems that can be fixed include:

- The wrong name and/or wrong address on the report
- A mistake, such as someone else's late payment being reported on your account
- Someone else's Social Security number on your report
- A foreclosure that never happened because you corrected your default
- A paid-off loan showing as still owed

Keep in mind that you can do all the correcting yourself by contacting the credit reporting bureaus and the lenders. However, it will take time and perseverance.

Bad Credit Factors That Usually Cannot Be Removed

- Filed bankruptcies
- Recorded legitimate foreclosures
- Late or missed payments
- Any kind of loan default

TIP

If you can't pay all of your bills, at least make your current mortgage payment. Remember, you're applying to a lender for a mortgage. How does it look if you can't make your current mortgage payments?

How Can a Borrower Correct a Credit Report Mistake?

My approach would be to first get evidence from the lender itself that an error has been made. Then I would write to the credit reporting agency offering the proof and demanding that the error be corrected. The credit reporting agency must investigate the request and take action, usually within a month.

Of course, getting a lender to acknowledge an error or even to acknowledge your letter or phone call can sometimes be difficult.

Nevertheless, persevere. In extreme cases having an attorney send a letter informing the lender that its error is causing you harm will do the trick.

If the original creditor reports that it made an error, the credit bureau will normally remove the offending report within 30 days.

If you can't get the lender to act in a timely fashion, you may be able to get the credit reporting agency to insert a letter of explanation along with the bad report. It may also make any substantiating documentation you have available to those who ask for reports.

Keep in mind, however, that credit bureaus don't take sides. In a disputed case, they probably will not remove the report. It may stay in your credit report for up to seven years.

Get a Copy of Your Credit Report

As noted earlier, it's a good idea to get a copy of your own credit report in advance of applying for a mortgage. That way you get to see what the lender will see and prepare for it. You are allowed to obtain one free copy of your credit report from each of the big three reporting agencies each year by going to the Web site: www.annualcreditreport.com.

You can also get your own credit report directly from each of the big three:

TransUnion, 800-916-8800, www.transunion.com
Experian (formerly TRW), 888-397-3742,
    www.experian.com
Equifax, 800-437-4619, www.equifax.com

How Can a Borrower Establish Credit If He or She Has None?

If you've never borrowed money and then repaid it, then you likely have no credit to show on your credit report. That's almost as bad as having bad credit. It provides no basis for making a credit judgment. Sometimes renters find themselves in this predicament.

There is, of course, a way out. At least six months to a year before you plan on applying for a mortgage, begin establishing a credit history.

Go to the bank where you do business (not having credit doesn't mean you don't have checking and savings accounts) and apply for a debit card. As you probably know, this is like a credit card, but it is based on your assets in the bank. Today many banks offer these almost automatically to their customers.

Once you have the debit card, use it frequently as a way of establishing that you can manage such an item. After a few months, ask your bank to establish an overdraft line of credit to cover your checking account.

Once you have an overdraft account and a debit account, ask your bank for a credit card. With your good standing in the bank, it should be automatic. Once you get that credit card, you're halfway home. Go out and charge something. When the bill comes, pay it promptly. Pay off all your charges each month for three months, and you will have established the beginnings of a credit history.

Apply for more cards (which should actually be arriving in the mail on their own), and get a personal loan from the bank. By the end of a year, you could have an extensive credit history.

Keep in mind, of course, that you don't want just to establish a credit history. You want a *good* credit history, and that means making all your payments on time.

Quick Ways to Establish a Credit History

You want to get a mortgage tomorrow, and you don't have a credit history. What do you do? Here are some tricks that you can use to let a lender know you pay your bills on time.

How to Assemble a Quick Credit History

- **Show your utility receipts.** As a tenant, you're probably paying for water, gas, garbage collection, cable TV, and more. You've paid by check so you have receipts. Also, the utility companies should be willing to issue you letters saying how well you've paid. This goes a long way toward establishing credit.

- **Don't forget your rent receipts.** If you paid your rent in cash, you got receipts from your landlord. Show those receipts to the lender, and get a letter of recommendation from your current landlord.

- **Loans from others.** Haven't you borrowed from friends or relatives? If so, didn't you pay it back on time? Get receipts and letters to prove it.

Getting a Cosigner

If you don't have good credit, get someone else who does to sign on the mortgage with you. (The lender may insist that the cosigner also be on the deed to the property.) Relatives and good friends are usually your best targets; however, even business associates are likely candidates.

TRAP

When someone cosigns with you, his or her credit is on the line. If you default, it will reflect badly on his or her credit. So keep in mind just what you're asking that person to do.

Also, keep in mind that if you put the cosigner on the deed as a purchaser (even though the cosigner didn't offer any money and will not be making the payments), a cosigner can tie up the property and potentially keep you from reselling. Be sure to have an attorney draw up an agreement specifying exactly what interests the cosigner actually has.

Buying Foreclosures

Whenever the real estate market cools down a bit, home buyers begin wondering if they should look into purchasing a foreclosure. (A *foreclosure* is a property that the owner has lost, or is losing, to a lender such as a bank.) Foreclosures have the reputation of being great deals—you pay less for the property and sometimes can get smaller monthly payments.

Are foreclosures a choice opportunity for renters? Or are they overhyped?

If you're a renter trying to find a way to convert the money you pay in rent into ownership, you should consider foreclosures. But you should also keep in mind that they are not an easy way in—they present an opportunity along with some fairly serious traps.

The Availability of Foreclosed Properties

At any given time there are hundreds of thousands of foreclosures on the real estate market across the country. As of this writing, this number is swelling, mainly due to high-risk financing that occurred over the last five years.

Over the past few years many buyers took out "option" and other low-monthly-payment ARMs where the interest not paid monthly was added to the back of the mortgage (see Chapter 6 and the Appendix). As a result, the initial monthly payments, frequently fixed for the first three to five years, were very low. However, now these loans are resetting at much higher interest rates with much higher monthly payments.

With a slower market, the owners find it difficult to resell. And with higher interest rates, refinancing also can be a problem. Hence they are forced into foreclosure. Here's a typical example:

High-Risk Financing

$300,000 mortgage
Teaser rate = 4 percent (market rate = 7 percent)
Monthly payment locked in for first 3 years = $1,000 (lost interest added to loan principal)
Monthly payment reset *after* first 3 years = $1,850
The low monthly payment of $1,000 automatically jumps up to $1,850 after the first 3 years, which is an increase of over 180 percent.

Hence, once the initial rate and payment reset, the borrower suddenly finds that his or her payment almost doubles. The borrower's alternatives are to pay the increased amount (which may simply not be possible), refinance to a new loan with another low teaser rate (which may not be available), sell, or lose the property. It's the last alternative that has caused so many foreclosures to come onto the market recently.

The Foreclosure Opportunity

The foreclosure process offers different opportunities at different times in the process . . . and different risks as well. In order to understand when you can buy and what the stakes are, it's important to understand the process.

While the foreclosure process varies state by state, there are three separate times at which you can buy the property during the foreclosure process:

1. When the lender notifies the borrower that he or she is in default but the borrower still owns the property (has the title); this is called "preforeclosure" by some.
2. When the trustee or court sells the property to the highest bidder (typically the lender) on the courthouse steps; this is the foreclosure sale.
3. When the lender has bought the property on the courthouse steps and now owns it and wants to get the property off its hands; this is referred to as a lender-owned, or real-estate-owned (REO), property.

TIP

There are two types of instruments broadly used for real estate loans in this country. The *traditional mortgage* is between a lender and a borrower, and it can be foreclosed only judicially, through court action. The second type of instrument is the *deed of trust*, and it involves not only the borrower and lender but also a trustee who actually holds the title. This instrument can be foreclosed far quicker than the traditional mortgage, and without going to court. Trust deeds are increasingly becoming the loan instrument of choice by lenders and are widely used on both coasts.

Buying during the Preforeclosure Stage

If a borrower doesn't make the payments on the mortgage, then the lender's ultimate recourse is to take back the property. This can be a long or short legal process, depending on your state. In states that use a trust deed, the process typically takes a little less than four months from the time the lender files the first "notice of default." In states with judicial foreclosure, it can be significantly longer (up to a year or more) from the time the lender files a notice of legal action until the property is "sold."

You can buy the property while it is in default from the borrower-owner, meaning the lender is foreclosing but hasn't yet taken the title. In this case, you would buy from the borrower-owner since she or he still has the title and can sell the property to you.

You will have a number of problems to deal with. You typically will have to arrange financing to pay off the existing defaulted mortgage as well as, perhaps, pay something to the seller. And you'll have to research the title to be sure just how many loans the seller has on the property, at what stage of foreclosure the property is in, and how much is actually owed.

It's a tricky time to buy the property.

TRAP

One of the worst things you can do is to take over the seller's defaulted mortgage only to later discover that the seller also has other mortgages on the property. Or that the property has *liens* on it from other lenders for the seller's bad debts. You could buy the property and end up owing more than its value!

Keep in mind that an owner who is in default on a mortgage still can usually save the property by making up the back payments, penalties, and interest. (In the final stages of foreclosure, the only way to save the property may be to refinance and pay off the defaulted mortgage.) Hence, that owner is likely to still want to negotiate some money from you for his or her equity.

The problem is that most owners who are defaulting on their mortgages don't realize how precarious their situation is. They want most of their equity out in cash while you, as a buyer, don't want to give them anything because they're about to lose their property anyway.

TIP

In most states the original borrower who is losing a property to foreclosure has an *equity of redemption* in which he or she may be able to come back and reclaim the title after a foreclosure sale. In some states this redemption might even apply after you buy the property from that person during the default period. This means that some time after you buy, fix up, and then try to resell the property, the original borrower-owner could come back, pay your costs (for purchasing), and take the property away from you!

It takes some delicate negotiations to mollify the seller as well as get you a deal that you'll be happy with. Which is why I say that buying at this stage can be tricky. My suggestion is that you always use a good agent and attorney when buying a property that's in default.

TRAP

There are numerous laws protecting seller-borrowers in default from overzealous investors. Be sure not to trip over them when buying during this preforeclosure stage.

It's important to understand that lenders are in the business of making loans, not taking back property through foreclosure. Almost always they will allow a borrower ample opportunity to make good on missed payments. Today lenders are usually required by the government to offer a payback plan designed to fit the borrower's needs and problems. Rarely will a lender begin foreclosure until the borrower is at least two to three months in arrears. Since it takes several additional months to complete the foreclosure process, you should have ample time to look into buying the property.

How Do I Find Properties in Default? They are advertised in *legal newspapers* (ones that carry legal notices) within the local county. Usually every major city has one. If your city does not have one, there are some other methods used to advertise legal notices. Check at the county courthouse and recorder's office to find out how it's done in your area.

You probably won't find the legal paper on the newsstand, and subscriptions can be expensive. On the other hand, there are a variety of Internet sites that offer information on properties in default including the following ones.

Internet Sites That Offer Information on Foreclosures

www.foreclosure.com

www.realtytrac.com

www.hud.gov/homes/homesforsale.cfm

Additionally, someone at a title insurance company may be able to quickly and easily supply all the information you need. (It is, after all, public information.)

How Do I Make an Offer on a Property in the Preforeclosure Stage? You'll usually have to do the investigation to find the property yourself, although a good agent may alert you to such deals. Once you identify a suitable property, you'll need to contact the owner and the lender(s) to find out exactly what's owed against the property. It's a good idea to get a condition of title report to ferret out all the mortgages and liens, some of which the seller may not mention or even know about.

Then you need to negotiate a price with the seller. Keep in mind that a property in default usually commands less-than-market price. You'll need to have an agent give you a *comparative market analysis* (CMA) so you will know what other similar properties have recently sold for. Of course, the amount of discount you'll demand and get will depend on your and your agent's abilities as negotiators.

TRAP

Sometimes properties in default are not listed. Hence, either you'll have to do all of the work yourself or pay a buyer's agent directly. The sellers may not want to or be able to pay an agent's commission themselves.

Before you make an offer, be sure to have it checked out by an attorney to see that you are protected and that you're in compliance with your state's laws regarding buying a property from a borrower in default.

To repeat, there are many tricks and traps when buying this way. For example, have your attorney find out if the borrower has filed for bankruptcy. (Many facing foreclosure do.) If the borrower has filed, he or she may not be able to sell you the property without court approval. The seller-borrower may not know this, or he or she may forget to mention it when you're negotiating a purchase.

Also, keep in mind that you may be able to negotiate good financing with the lender. Talk to the lender. It may be willing to let you assume the existing mortgage, or even give you a new and higher one if you agree to pay the current interest rate and make up the back payments. After all, you'll be solving a big problem for the lender.

Buying on the Courthouse Steps

The second opportunity to buy a property in foreclosure is when the court or the trustee sells it to the highest bidder "on the courthouse steps." (Don't laugh; many times this is quite literal—the deal is done on the steps.)

Again, the time and date of the sale are advertised in a legal paper. And some Internet sites, such as those mentioned above, can help you with this.

Keep in mind that the lender is almost certainly going to be there and is going to bid the remaining amount of the mortgage *plus* any accrued interest and penalties. To buy the property, you'll have to bid higher.

TRAP

The biggest danger at this stage is that the property may have more than one mortgage on it, and the holders of the other mortgages may not be at the auction. You could buy the property paying off the existing loan only to later discover that what you thought was seller's equity was actually covered by other mortgages. In other words, you could be buying a pig in a poke—paying too much. Be sure that you've thoroughly researched the property through a title search so that you'll know what mortgages are on it.

Buying at auction is also tricky. You should not attempt it yourself, at least not the first time around. Get an agent who's done it many times before to guide you. And also be sure your attorney checks out the purchase, the property, and the title.

Buying from the Lender

In most cases the lender is the one who buys the property on the courthouse steps. After all, it has the full value of the mortgage (plus back interest and penalties) to apply to the purchase price.

The last opportunity to get the property in foreclosure, and usually the *least* risky for you, involves now buying the property not from the original borrower-owner, but from the lender.

Lender-Owned Properties

Lender-owned properties are called real-estate-owned (REO) properties. The term refers to properties that are owned by lenders, such as banks, or large institutions like Fannie Mae, Freddie Mac, or other organizations. For them, REOs are undesirable things. Their purpose is to lend money, not to own property. Having to take property through foreclosure indicates a failure of their lending practices. Hence, they are usually very anxious to get rid of these properties. (They show up as liabilities instead of assets on their books.)

By the way, the term *real-estate-owned (REO) property* means any property taken back through foreclosure and owned by a lender. Properties owned by the federal government are usually called *government repossessions* (or *government repos*).

REOs, unfortunately, are frequently run-down, derelict properties. After all, why should the former owner have bothered to keep the property up when he or she was about to lose it to foreclosure? The windows may all be broken, there could be holes in the walls, there could be rooms gutted by fires set by vandals, and so on. Although most lenders will make an effort to protect the properties during the default stage, sometimes there's little they can do. Thus, be sure you physically check out any REO. It may be in such bad shape you won't want it.

Fixed-Up REOs

Sometimes the lender will spend the money necessary to put the REO in tip-top shape. The problem, here, is that when this is done, the lender typically lists the property with a broker and then tries to get top dollar for it. This is usually not an opportunity for you to get in with a lower price and, consequently, lower payments. Sometimes the lender, however, will offer more favorable terms such as a smaller down payment or a lower interest rate to get buyers interested in the property.

Finding REOs

Here, again, you'll need to do most of the work yourself, although sometimes an agent can do much of it for you. Go into a local bank branch and ask for their REO department. However, don't expect to be politely escorted to a big department and treated as an important client. Rather, you'll probably be told either that the lender has no REOs, meaning it's in great financial shape, or that all the REOs it has are listed with such and such real estate agency and you'll need to check with them (and pay full market price).

That's not necessarily the case. The lender may have many REOs that are in bad shape and may not want to admit it to anyone who simply walks in off the street.

On the other hand, if you're a depositor (particularly if you have substantial funds deposited) or are a stockholder with that bank, then the lender's people may feel obliged to talk with you. Or if you present yourself as a person ready, willing, and able to buy, you may also get a hearing.

What you want to get from a bank or other lender is the name of the officer who handles REOs. Who's in charge of the REO department? If you're successful, what you'll often get is a written list of addresses with prices. Those are the lender's REOs, and now it's up to you to check them out.

Making an Offer on an REO

Once you find a property you're interested in, you'll make an offer either directly to the lender or through its agent. Your offer is similar to what you'll make on any property. But you must be sure that you include specific demands such as the following.

Demands to Include in Your REO Offer

- **Title insurance.** You want to know that you will end up with a clear title to the property.
- **Financing.** You want to be sure that either the REO lender will finance the property or you've got your own lender to finance the deal.

- **Clean-up.** If the property isn't spotless, you'll want an allowance to have it cleaned, or a lower price to justify taking on the mess.

Sometimes, your best chance of getting a good REO deal is directly with the lender's REO officer. Make an appointment, sit down with him or her, and say that you want to buy the property (which you've already scouted out) on the particular terms you are listing for the officer. If you're dealing with the person who has the power to make a sell decision, you could walk out with the property.

If you're dealing with a lender, remember that everything is negotiable . . . depending. It all depends on how desperate the lender is to get rid of the particular property and how much money the lender has in it. (No lender wants to sell for less than the former mortgage amount plus back interest, penalties, and costs, although in desperate times, some lenders will do just that.)

Keep in mind that the costs of fixing up the property are negotiable too. An REO office may want to dump the property, and it might give you anywhere from $10,000 to $50,000 on the spot either in the form of a price reduction or a fix-up allowance.

To get the best deal, know what you want to give for price, terms, repairs, and so on. Then negotiate to find out what the most is that the lender is willing to give. If you're new to negotiating, I suggest you try my *Tips and Traps When Negotiating Real Estate*, Second Edition (McGraw-Hill, 2005). It has many techniques that work on foreclosures.

The Risks Involved in Buying an REO

Frequently such REO sales are *as is*. This means that no matter what problems the property has, they're yours. Further, the lender may not know what those problems are—hence, you won't get much from the seller's disclosures.

This means you need to conduct a thorough inspection. Hire a good inspector . . . or two.

TRAP

Property inspectors usually report only on what they can see. If a cracked floor is covered by a carpet, or if structural damage is contained within a wall, or if there's mold hidden under floorboards, they may not find it. A brief inspection may not turn up real problems in a property, especially a foreclosure.

Also, there could be an occupant in the property. This could be the former borrower-owner or a tenant. In any event, getting the occupant out could be an expensive and lengthy process. I always put into my REO offers that it's the responsibility of the lender to see that the property is vacant when I take possession. Lenders are in a far better position than you (with their lawyers) to handle this problem.

Finally, sometimes the lender won't be able to give you a clear title. It could be locked up in litigation, probate, bankruptcy, or some other problem. If this happens, it might be a good idea to just pass on the property.

Are REOs the Best Foreclosure Opportunity?

Yes and no. They're usually the cleanest deals. On the other hand, they usually don't afford as big a bargain as buying at other times.

It's a case of risk versus gain.

If you want to buy a property that may offer minimal cash and lower interest rates and lower monthly payments but are willing to accept the chance that it might not all work out in the end, try foreclosures.

Bidding Low for Bargain Buys

Let's face it—homes are expensive, *very* expensive. These days, experiencing sticker shock when looking to buy is not uncommon.

One way to make a home more affordable is to cut the price—to pay less than the seller is asking. For each $10,000 less in price you pay on a home when interest rates are running at 7 percent, you will save yourself about $75 a month (principal, interest, taxes, and insurance). Cut the price by $40,000 and you've reduced your monthly payment by approximately $300. That could be the difference between being able to afford the property . . . and not.

Of course, that's not to mention the cuts you'll also have made in your down payment and closing costs, most of which are calculated as a percentage of the purchase price. As a renter looking to buy, getting a price reduction should be one of your main goals.

Further, when you pay less, you increase the likelihood of making a profit when you later resell. Nothing makes more sense than buying low and eventually selling high.

As a buyer, it's a good practice to not simply always offer the asking price. Consider offering less . . . sometimes much less. You might "steal" the property and end up with very low payments and little cash invested.

But how do you arrange to pay less for a house? If the seller is asking $500,000 for the property, how do you negotiate that price down to $475,000? Or even $450,000? Or $350,000?

In this chapter we're going to look at some of the techniques used to get a better price when you buy. They can benefit any buyer at any time.

The Art of Lowballing

When you offer what the seller is asking (or close to it), it's sometimes called "making a fair offer." When you offer far less than the asking price, it's called "lowballing the seller."

The implication is that lowballing is not fair. Nothing could be further from the truth.

You're entitled to offer whatever you want when you make an offer. Yet real estate agents will often suggest that you offer as close as possible to what the seller is asking. They may say that's only *fair*. The implication is that the asking price is at market and you should pay market price for the property.

Why do agents do this?

As a buyer, you should be looking out for yourself first. Your goal is to get as good a deal for you as you can, without cheating. After all, the only reason the sellers will agree to a good deal for you, presumably, is because it's also a good deal for them. That's a win-win situation.

Reasons Given for Offering Close to the Asking Price

There are usually two reasons that agents have for suggesting that you offer as close to the asking price as possible. The first reason is what they tell you outright: it's that the closer to the asking price you offer, the more likely your chance of getting your offer accepted. If the sellers are asking $250,000 and you offer $245,000, it's almost a slam dunk. Few sellers will turn away an offer that's only 2 percent less than they're asking. (The exception is in a very hot market when properties sometimes sell for *more* than their asking price!) This is perfectly true.

The other reason is seldom expressed. It's that it's far harder for the agent to get a lowball offer accepted than a "fair" one. Ask yourself, how hard does the agent have to work to get the seller to knock five grand off the price? On the other hand, how hard does the agent have to work to get the seller to knock $50,000 or even $100,000 off?

The truth is that many agents are lousy negotiators. They do their real selling on you, the buyer, by getting you to offer high. Then it's easy getting the sellers to accept.

From your perspective, however, you want the agent to be doing it the other way around—to be doing the real selling on the sellers, getting them to accept your lowball offer. After all, think how foolish and unsatisfied you'll feel if you make a "fair" offer, only to always suspect you could have gotten the home for far less.

Should You Always Lowball?

On the other hand, when you lowball a seller, you run the risk of not getting the property. Sometimes sellers will be offended by a lowball offer. As a result, they won't do the one thing that you hope they'll do: *counter your offer.*

If you offer $50,000 below the asking price, while you may entertain some fantasies of getting the home for that price, your real goal is probably to get the sellers to come back (counteroffer) at a price lower than they are asking. From there you can begin negotiations toward a more acceptable (to you) price.

For example, the sellers are asking $400,000. You offer $300,000. Now the seller counters at $350,000, splitting the difference and hoping you'll accept.

Consider what you've done. Your lowball offer has gotten the seller to come down $50,000, or over 12 percent. If you had originally offered $350,000, chances are the sellers would still have split the difference, and you'd have had a counteroffer of $375,000. Thus your lowball got the seller to come down further, and by continuing to negotiate, the seller might come down even more.

TRAP

Some buyers feel that if the sellers will come down on a lowball offer, why not offer a deeper lowball to get them down even more? The reason is that beyond a certain point, which only the sellers know, they'll simply walk away from the table and refuse to negotiate.

On the other hand, the sellers could be "insulted" by your lowball offer. They may simply say "No" and refuse to enter into any further negotiations.

What do you do now?

If you really love the house, your only alternative is to come back with a higher offer. But having once been rebuffed at a lowball price, your higher offer is likely to also be rebuffed. The seller, with some justification, may feel that you simply don't know how to negotiate and the best way to deal with you is to hang tough at the original price.

Thus, the big risk of lowballing is that you'll lose out on a good deal. Indeed, you might lose out on the home itself if the sellers refuse to come down on price at all and you can't, or won't, pay the full price. Thus, you should *not always* lowball. Do it when you feel you can afford to lose the house, or when you sense the seller is anxious to sell and may make a big price concession.

The Effect of Market Conditions on Lowballing

It's important to understand that the chances of getting a lowball offer accepted are determined not only by the seller's own needs and emotions but also by market conditions.

If the market is strong and there are three buyers behind you ready to make offers, no lowball offer is likely to be taken seriously. After all, the sellers can easily afford to say no and wait for the next buyer's offer.

On the other hand, if the market is weak and the house has been for sale for four or five months with no offers, it's a different story. Here your lowball offer is sure to at least be seriously considered. After all, if the sellers turn it down, how do they know anyone else will soon make another offer?

TIP Lowball offers work best in a weak housing market, and they work poorly in a strong market.

You might reasonably expect to take a chance on a lowball offer in a weak market while you offer high in a strong market. All of which is to say, know what the market is like before you make your offer.

How Do You Know What the Market Conditions Are?

Any good real estate agent can tell what the market conditions are like. To be sure, however, you should check reports in local media about the housing market. The media just love to report when prices are rising or falling. If there are no reports, chances are the market is simply stagnant.

You should also check the *inventory* of unsold houses in your area. Statistics on this are kept by local real estate boards, and they are made available through participating agents. Any time the inventory of unsold homes drops below a month's supply, the market is overheated. On the other hand, if the inventory is more than six months old, it is a very cold market.

Most normal markets have an unsold inventory of around three or four months' supply of homes.

How Do You Know What the Home Is Really Worth?

Before making any lowball offers, you need to know the true value of the property. You can usually find this out from a *comparative market analysis* (CMA).

Since homes rarely sell for their listed price, you should get a list of the *actual selling prices* of comparable homes, called the *comps*.

Any good agent can provide these. Ask your agent to let you see the selling prices of comps going back at least a year.

From the list, pick out all sales for similar houses, and then try to get as close a match as possible (same or similar square footage, number of bedrooms, bathrooms, location, amenities, and so on). Expect to find half a dozen sales or more in most markets.

Next, you'll need to subtract for features that the comps have that your subject house doesn't. And add for features your subject house has that the comps don't.

Don't try to add on to the price the full cost of any remodeling the seller may have done. Typically most remodeling projects return only about half their cost. A new kitchen or bathroom, however, can return up to 100 percent of their cost, if the remodeling was done well, it was an older property now brought up to modern standards, and the property now meets the norms of the neighborhood.

Beware of homes that are overremodeled. Any house that's priced more than 5 percent above its neighbors because of improvements may be a *white elephant*—a home that's been over-improved for the neighborhood.

Deciding How Deep Your Lowball Offer Should Be

Once you know the true value of the home, based on a CMA, you can make your offer decision.

It's easy if the home is significantly overpriced. You can simply offer the market value (or below), and the agent who presents the offer can point out all the comps to prove the appropriateness of the price offered.

On the other hand, if the house is fairly priced, it's harder to make a lowball offer and hope to get it accepted. Generally speaking, at such times the reason for sellers to accept a lowball is because of their own special circumstances.

Keep in mind that most sellers ask for more than they are actually willing to take for their homes. They are expecting to come down some. (That's why paying what the seller is asking often is simply wasting money, even if the seller is right at market.) But why would a seller take far less?

The seller may be *highly motivated* to sell, meaning desperate, for any number of reasons including some of the following.

Factors That Can Highly Motivate a Seller

- The seller's job change is necessitating an immediate move from the area.
- The seller has bought a new home and has two mortgage payments.
- The seller has bought a new home, and the purchase is contingent on the sale of this home.

- The seller is in the midst of getting a divorce, and the settlement has demanded the sale of the home.
- The seller has lost his or her job or has an illness requiring downsizing his or her expenses (that is, he or she cannot continue to make the payments).
- The seller desires to move to a bigger (or smaller) home because of a change in his or her family size.
- The seller is retiring, which is mandating a downsizing to save on monthly payments and to get cash out of the home.
- The seller is tired of living in his or her existing home or neighborhood and wants a change.

Note, the above list goes from top to bottom in terms of motivation. The top reasons are generally the most highly motivating, and the bottom are often the least.

Thus, what motivates your seller, as well as the market, will help determine how likely he or she is to accept (or come close to) your lowball offer. The question now becomes, how do you learn what the seller's motivation actually is?

Finding Out What May Be Motivating the Seller

One way is to simply ask the sellers, "Why are you selling?"

You can do this when you tour the house if the sellers happen to be home. I'm always amazed at how candid many sellers will be when asked this question.

Another way is to ask your agent (or their agent, if available). Generally speaking, agents are not supposed to reveal the sellers' motivation unless the sellers tell them it's okay. Many agents, however, are simply garrulous and will spill the beans if you ask.

Yet another method is to simply go around to the neighbors. Explain you're looking to buy the home next door. Ask them if

they can tell you anything about the home. Some will simply bubble over with useful information about the home and the sellers.

Another way to find out is with a lowball trial offer. If it's
accepted, you know the sellers were highly motivated. Doing this,
however, as we've seen, risks losing the house.

Very often a seller, when faced with a lowball offer, will come down
only a few thousand dollars. They are simply saying, yes, I'm willing to
negotiate. But I'm not willing to give a deep discount on my price. If
this happens, you can decide whether or not to pursue it further, but
it's unlikely you'll ultimately get the house at a lowball price.

The Steps in the Lowballing Process

It all starts out with a very low bid. After all, you can't very well go
lower after you've previously made a high bid—that would cost
you your credibility.

However, if you bid *too low,* as we've noted, the sellers may be
insulted. They may believe you're just playing with them, that
you're not really interested in buying the property. As a result, they
may simply turn your offer down without making a counteroffer.
Which means you could lose out if you really want the house.

Thus, you need to bid high enough to keep the sellers interested. Yet low enough to get yourself a bargain. Just what is that
magic number?

I've been asked that question many times. Mostly the question
is in the form of a request to come up with a numerical figure. Is
it 5 percent? 10 percent? 15? 25? 50? "How much lower than the
asking price should I offer?"

My answer is, "Know thyself." In other words, the answer is,
how much are you willing to risk?

To figure out just where you stand, I've found a 5-point evaluation scale is helpful. Ask yourself where you are on this scale.

Personal Evaluation Scale

5. I'll simply die if I don't get this house.
4. This is a great house for the family.
3. This is one of the best homes I've seen.
2. This house mostly fits our needs.
1. I don't care if I get this house or not.

If you're a 5, you don't have much negotiation room. If you're a 1, by all means make a ridiculously lowball offer.

> **TIP**
>
> From an investment perspective, it's better to lowball 10 houses and not get any of them than to pay too much for 1 house. From a personal perspective, don't lowball a house that you can't stand to live without.

If you're looking at the property as a home in which to live, your tolerance for risk may be low. This is particularly the case if you've "fallen in love with the house." You simply may not be able to handle not getting it.

If that's the case, then I suggest you throw in the towel even before negotiations start. You have no negotiation position. Simply pay full price (or close to it) and get the misery over with.

On the other hand, if you're willing to stand back and look at the property objectively, it's a different story. If you can say to yourself, "If I don't get this house, there'll always be another," you have a much greater tolerance for risk. And a lowball offer is probably in order.

What to Do If Your Agent Does Not Want to Convey Your Lowball Offer

The simple answer is, get a better agent.

Some agents are terrible negotiators, and they know it. They'll refuse to take a lowball offer because they know they'll have trouble getting it accepted. They'll whine and try to get you to submit a "fair" offer.

Keep in mind the seller's agent has to take every legitimate offer to the seller (unless the seller has specifically said not to bring in offers below a certain level, which almost never happens). A legitimate offer is one that is in writing with a deposit. Your agent may not like it, but he or she should do it.

On the other hand, if yours is the kind of agent who is unhappy making a lowball offer, you're probably better off looking elsewhere. Your best bet is finding that agent who sees the lowball offer as a challenge, one he or she is eager to accept.

TIP

One reason for using a *buyer's agent*, one who represents you and not the seller, is that it's that agent's duty to get the best price for you, the buyer. An agent who represents the sellers, on the other hand, has a duty to get the best price for them. (Most buyer's agents still get paid by the seller—ask them.)

Can I Call the Seller? Why not? You can even present your offer directly to the seller. However, most agents don't encourage you to talk to the seller. That bypasses the agent and probably makes them suspect you're trying to avoid paying a commission.

If you feel the need to talk to the seller, do so—the seller is only a phone call away. On the other hand, some sellers are reticent to talk directly to buyers. They'd rather the agent handle all the negotiations. Of course, you won't know unless you ask.

Appraisal Offers

One seldom-used approach is to make an offer contingent upon an appraisal. You and the seller agree to accept as the sales price whatever price the appraiser comes up with. (Agents can almost always put you in touch with an appraiser, and the cost is usually around $350.)

If the seller goes along, you'll agree to accept whatever a professional appraiser says the property is worth. (Typically such offers include top and bottom limits on the price.)

This is a technique sometimes used on investment properties, but rarely with houses. However, if you have a seller who's hung up on price and just won't come down . . . and if you're convinced the house is priced way above market, you might consider it. Just keep in mind, however, that when you bring in a third party, even an appraiser, it's like rolling dice. You never know what the results will be. You could end up with a great price . . . or a terrible one.

Lowball offers are one way of getting into a home that you could not otherwise afford. And such offers can sometimes create a terrific opportunity to buy a home at a bargain price with less cash and lower monthly payments.

FSBOs and First-Time-Buyer Programs

Another means of buying a home with a lower price and lower payments is to buy it directly from the seller and avoid the agents. These properties are called *for sale by owner*, or FSBO (pronounced "fizbo").

The hope with a FSBO is that, since the seller is not using an agent and isn't paying upwards of 6 percent in sales commissions, he or she will pass all or part of that savings on to you. For example, if the home costs $500,000 and the seller is saving a 6 percent commission, the amount is $30,000. If that savings were passed on to you, you could buy the home for $470,000, and $30,000 off a 7 percent mortgage for 30 years is a savings of over $200 monthly.

Thus, looking for FSBOs can make a lot of sense. Be forewarned, however, that you'll be dealing directly with sellers and that not all sellers have the expertise to handle a sale. And all too often they have an inflated idea of the value of the property. Thus, even though you might save on the commission, the house might be so overpriced as to negate that bonus.

TRAP

About 85 percent of sellers who start out trying to sell FSBO eventually give up and list the property with an agent. The difficulties FSBO sellers confront trying to sell their property on their own can be advantageous to a buyer whose offer may be the only real opportunity at a sale the FSBO seller may have had in weeks or months.

Making an Offer to a FSBO Seller

When you're working with an agent, presumably that agent will handle the paperwork and see that it's done right. When you make an offer directly to a seller by yourself, it's up to you to see that it is handled correctly. Therefore, here are three methods you can use to make an offer to a FSBO seller and to handle the subsequent documentation:

1. **Use a buyer's agent.** There is no reason you can't use an agent to write up and present an offer to a FSBO seller. It's done all the time. Very often FSBO sellers are willing to pay a 3 percent buyer's agent's commission, so it won't cost you anything out of pocket. (Note, however, that if the seller won't pay the agent's fee, then it will be up to you to pay it.) Usually you would ask the FSBO seller if he or she will *cobroke* the property. That's asking the seller if he or she will work with a broker. Any smart FSBO seller will agree. Then you ask the seller how much of a commission he or she will pay. If it's the usual going rate for a broker bringing in a buyer, you're in business. Have your agent put the deal together, including all the paperwork, at the seller's expense.

2. **Use an attorney.** On the East Coast many attorneys are set up to handle real estate transactions. Their typical fee

is a bargain and is anywhere from $500 to $1,500, depending on the size and complexity of the transaction. They will prepare all the necessary paperwork and in some cases, even handle the escrow. On the West Coast and in the Midwest, you'll have more difficulty finding a real estate attorney, and his or her services will likely cost more.

3. **Try a fee-for-service agent.** Here the agent does specific work, such as prepare the purchase agreement, for a set fee, say, $500 or $1,000. Many agents who advertise that they will discount their commission will also perform fee-for-service work.

Handling the Paperwork Involved in Purchasing a FSBO Property

Keep in mind that most people selling FSBO will already have addressed the problem of paperwork. They probably have an attorney or agent waiting in the wings to do it for the both of you. Just be sure the person they choose is competent and professional. (You probably don't want the paperwork handled by the seller's brother-in-law whose claim to expertise is that he's bought and sold three houses.)

TRAP

Don't attempt to do the paperwork yourself unless you're very well versed in real estate law. This is an area that tolerates no mistakes. The wrong language, a mis-interpretation of a rule, the failure to include some important item such as your demand for a professional home inspection—any of these and many others could result in a bad deal that could end up in litigation. You want the paperwork done right so have a professional do it.

If there's no agent involved, but just you and the seller, one or both of you have to do the work. Get an initial understanding between you and the seller on the delegation of responsibilities. Make sure you know who is doing what.

How to Close a FSBO Deal

- Be sure you're preapproved and have the necessary financing to complete the purchase. Make sure the deal is contingent on getting a mortgage that you need and that the property has been appraised for enough for you to make the purchase.
- Find an escrow-title insurance company and open escrow.
- Get a professional home inspection. Make sure your approval is a condition of purchase. Give your approval if the inspection says the property is okay, or order additional reports. If there's repair work to be done, be sure it gets done (usually repairs are paid for by the seller). Read the inspection report and negotiate any repairs.
- Today, getting a copy of claims the seller has made against the home insurer over the last five years is sometimes also done. Be sure your approval here is also a condition of sale.
- Be sure the seller gets a termite clearance. Any repair work required because of termite damage is usually paid for by the seller. This should be part of all purchase agreements as you won't normally get financing without a termite clearance.
- Get any other inspections or reports that are commonly done in your area. For example, on the West Coast a seismic report is often required.
- Be sure the seller gives you a disclosure statement and that your approval of it is a condition of your purchase. Read it carefully, and challenge any entries that show problems. For example, you may want to insist that the seller complete certain repairs, or you may want to renegotiate the price or even back out of the deal.

- Read and accept or reject any and all inspection reports and disclosures.
- Arrange a final walk-through so that you can be sure the seller hasn't damaged the property during the escrow period.
- Be sure to get adequate title insurance to protect your interest in the property.
- Have your lender send funds to close the deal.
- Get the key and move in.

If you and the seller split the workload, there's not that much to be done in a typical deal. And having an agent or attorney handle the technical aspects is really a plus.

Negotiating Tips for Dealing Face-to-Face with the Seller

For most people, negotiating directly with the seller without the intermediary broker is really tough. Most of us are too willing to give up more than we need to, and we are not tough enough to get the best deal. Here are some negotiating tips that you may find useful.

1. Never Argue; Always Discuss. If you argue with the seller, what probably began as a small disagreement can quickly escalate because there's no third party to calm down the argument. You could each end up in a rigid, uncompromising position that would make consummating a deal impossible.

Instead, simply listen to the seller and then present your position. If you're at odds, then look for common ground and whittle away until you're both in agreement. Sound easier than it is? Perhaps, but with a little practice and keeping a cool head, it works surprisingly well.

And remember not to make it personal. Whether or not you get the property is not an ego thing. Whether you get the best possible deal is simply to your advantage. As a result, never say anything personally disparaging to the seller. To do so will almost immediately end the negotiations. If the seller says something personal to you, make note of it, and then move on. If you hold it personally against the seller, again the deal's likely off.

2. Don't Try to Be the Seller's Friend. We all want to deal with friends, people whom we believe we can trust. Sellers are no different. If the sellers like you, you've got a better chance of making the deal. But if you try to make the sellers like you, chances are they'll see through your strategy and see you as a shallow, callous person. Not a good thing. Just be yourself. If the sellers happen to like you, all the better.

3. Use Facts and Figures That Everyone Can Agree On. Sellers often have inflated ideas of what their property is worth. You may know it's only worth $250,000. But they may be convinced it's actually worth $300,000. When you suggest the figure may be a bit high, they point out all the money, sweat, and time they put into the property.

Be polite, but tell the sellers simply that they're being unrealistic. Hopefully you've done your homework and you can point to a list of recent comparable sales. Let the facts do the work for you. Simply begin reading down the list. A similar property on Johnston Street sold for $242,000 last month. Four months ago a similarly located property on Maple Street sold for $260,000. Three weeks ago escrow closed on a property just like theirs for $250,000. Figures don't lie. They tell what the house is worth.

If you tell the sellers they are unrealistic and back it up with facts, one of two things will happen. Either they'll agree and you'll have a deal at a price you can afford, or they'll simply reject what you say and throw you out. Which is okay because at least you'll have saved yourself from wasting any more time on a hopeless negotiation.

4. Always Be Truthful. Never tell a lie, not even a tiny, little, small one. If you have a credit problem, you don't necessarily have to bring it up. (Although if it's going to affect the deal, getting it out in the open early on is a good idea.) However, once it comes up, don't lie about it. Don't make it bigger than it is, but don't make it smaller either.

Lies, even small ones, have a way of poisoning the negotiation. If the seller catches you in a lie, he or she begins wondering what else you're lying about. Maybe your whole presentation is a lie? Maybe you're just there to cheat the seller? Maybe you really don't have the cash to buy or can't qualify for the mortgage? And on and on. Telling the truth may hurt, but it hurts a lot less than lying.

5. Try My Book. For more hints on negotiating real estate transactions, look into *Tips and Traps When Negotiating Real Estate*, Second Edition (McGraw-Hill, 2005).

The Importance of Getting the Purchase Agreement in Writing

According to the Statute of Frauds, all transactions for real property must be in writing. It doesn't usually matter what the sellers say—it's what they put down in black and white that counts.

Get your agent or attorney or whoever is doing the paperwork to draw up an agreement as quickly as possible that reflects the terms of your purchase. Then get the sellers' signature on it.

Remember, agreement is often a fleeting thing. You may be agreed now, but come tomorrow morning, the sellers may have second thoughts. It's too late if it's in writing. But if the agreement is only verbal, you may have to start negotiations all over again.

Finding FSBO Sellers

Check your local newspapers under the "real estate for sale" heading, "by owner." Check the Internet. There are dozens if not hundreds of FSBO sites. Walk the streets in the neighborhoods that interest you. You may find a FSBO sign in the next block.

TIP When you're serious about a property, don't simply breeze in, make an offer, and then breeze out. Plan to spend time with the sellers. The more time you invest with the sellers, the better your chance of getting the deal you want.

Special First-Time-Buyer Programs

Let's change gears for a moment and consider yet another way of getting into a home cheaply. This applies only if you're a first-time buyer.

A *first-time buyer* is not, as you might suppose, someone who's never bought a home. Instead, the term usually refers to someone who hasn't bought or owned a home for the past 3 years. If you bought a home 10 years ago, sold it 5 years ago, and have been a renter since, then you should qualify as a first-time buyer.

There are dozens of first-time programs designed specifically to make homes more affordable to people presently renting homes or apartments. These programs typically offer aid with the down payment or the monthly payment or both.

Most such programs, however, are operated by cities or counties. That means that in order to find them, you'll have to do some digging on your own.

In order to apply for them, you usually must contact the office of the housing director (or whatever other name your city or county uses). When you do, you'll be told of the type of program available, the qualifications, and how to apply for it.

In order to get into the program, you'll usually need to get a certificate of qualification. To get this, not only must you be a first-time buyer but very frequently you must also have a low income for your family size.

The amount you can pay for the home and the maximum mortgage are also sometimes restricted. In some cases there are outright grants, while in others the government body will actually buy the home and then sell it to you over time.

There are on occasion other programs that cater to first-time buyers. Check with any local or Internet mortgage broker. Also check out these Web sites:

www.fanniemae.com
www.freddiemac.com
www.hud.gov

Understanding Real Estate Tax Advantages

Tax rules are always in a state of flux. They are changed by interpretations, IRS rulings, court precedents, new legislation, and more. The discussion in this chapter is designed to give you only an overview of the general nature of real estate taxation. Because of the changing nature of tax rules, you should not rely on this material. For tax advice you should consult with a tax professional.

Are Your Property Taxes Deductible?

As of this writing, they are. You can deduct the amount you pay in state property taxes on your personal residence from your federal and in most cases your state income taxes.

Is the Interest on Your Mortgage Deductible?

Generally speaking, yes, up to certain limits.

The amount of interest you can deduct on a home that you own and in which you live is limited. The limitations include these:

1. The maximum mortgage amount deducted can be $1 million, provided that the mortgage was used to purchase, build, or improve your home.
2. The deduction applies only to your principal residence and to a second home. If it's a second home, you must use it part of the year.
3. Any mortgage debt taken out prior to October 13, 1987, is grandfathered in.
4. If you take out a mortgage (refinance) on your home for purposes other than to improve, build, or add on, you are limited to $100,000 of debt on which interest may be deducted.

The rule is tricky. You may purchase a home with a mortgage of $300,000. Under the rule, all of the interest on this mortgage is presumably deductible. After you buy the property, you decide to add to the house and secure a mortgage for $250,000 more. If the money is used to build or improve the property, all the interest on the second mortgage is likewise deductible.

However, if you took out a second on the same property for $250,000 and used the money to start a business of your own, only the interest on the first $100,000 of the debt would be deductible.

Also, if you take out a mortgage against your home and then buy bonds that are tax free or otherwise receive tax-free income, the interest on the mortgage may not be deductible.

On the other hand, there may be a special exception available to you if you use the money for education. Check with your accountant.

As I said, mortgage interest in general is deductible, but . . . Be sure you check with any accountant or other tax professional to see what the circumstances are in your case.

Are the Points You Pay When You Buy a Home Deductible?

Points are usually a form of prepaid interest. These fees are paid up front when you get the loan. Points are usually deductible but not necessarily all in the same year.

If the points truly represent prepaid interest, then you may be able to deduct them. However, you probably must deduct them over the life of the mortgage. If the mortgage is for 30 years, then the deduction for points must be spread out over that period of time. For example, two points on a $200,000 mortgage for 30 years are deductible at $133 a year.

There is an exception to the above rule that allows you to deduct points in the year you pay them providing you meet certain criteria.

You Can Deduct Points in the Year You Purchase the House If . . .

- The mortgage is used to purchase your principal residence. It must be used for buying or improving that residence. You cannot deduct points in the year you paid them on a mortgage for a second residence, even though interest on that mortgage may be deductible. You may, however, be able to deduct the points over the life of the mortgage on the second home.

   Your principal residence is generally the place where you spend most of your time. Unless you spend more than 50 percent of your time there, though, it might be hard to prove that a house is your principal residence.
- You pay the points out of your own funds. The points are not paid out of the money loaned to you by the lender. This issue comes into play when the lender rolls your clos-ing costs into the mortgage.

TIP

Some borrowers have taken to writing a separate check to the lender to cover the cost of the points. In this way they have a paper record of having paid for them separately from funds advanced by the lender.

- The amount of points charged must be customary for the area. If you "buy down" a mortgage (by paying additional points up front), the government may determine that the points you paid were in excess of what is customary for your area and disallow the deduction in the year paid.
- The points cannot be the fees paid for appraisals, credit reports, or the origination fees charged for FHA loans or special fees charged for VA loans.
- The points must represent interest. The deductions are applicable only if the points do not exceed the maximum interest deduction allowable on a residence.

TRAP

If you are purchasing or refinancing a rental property, different rules apply. There, you may deduct the points only over the life of the mortgage; however, you may also be able to deduct your other costs and fees as a business expense. Check with your accountant.

Determining which, if any, points are deductible can be tricky. You should discuss it with your tax professional before actually taking the deduction on your taxes.

How Valuable Is Mortgage Interest as a Tax Deduction?

Today, all personal interest is nondeductible. That means that interest expenses on your car loans, credit cards, department store charges, and so forth are not deductible. (They may be deductible as a business expense if you own your own business, but that's a separate issue.)

Mortgage interest, up to the limits noted earlier, is deductible. For this reason, many people opt to borrow on a home equity loan for their personal financing needs.

However, you should be wary of home equity mortgages that are sold on the basis of their tax deductibility. Often times the lender really doesn't know whether or not such a mortgage would benefit you from a tax perspective. It could turn out that the interest on the loan isn't tax deductible when you thought it was.

Late payments on a mortgage are generally deductible if they constitute interest. If they are for a specific service that the lender performs, such as sending out late-payment notices, they probably are not deductible.

What about Interest Added to a Mortgage?

We're talking about negative amortization, as discussed in Chapter 6. Generally speaking, you can't deduct interest unless you pay it. By converting it to principal, as in negative amortization, it presumably stops being interest. You may, however, be able to deduct the extra interest incurred because of the additional principal.

If the mortgage is in truth a personal loan (which is sometimes the case on that portion of a mortgage given for more than 100 percent of the LTV ratio), the interest on the amount deemed a personal loan may not be deductible. This is one of the great traps with 125 percent mortgages.

What Are the Tax Consequences of Refinancing?

Generally speaking, there usually aren't any immediate tax consequences of refinancing except that you may have more interest to deduct—see above. For tax purposes, the amount of financing on a home is basically irrelevant when it comes to capital gains taxes.

What Are the Tax Consequences When You Sell?

Right now your enthusiasm is probably up for a purchase. The last thing on your mind may be selling. But good tax planning requires that you know what the rules are well in advance. You might sell in eight years, or next year, and in either scenario, the tax consequences, as we'll see, could be dramatically different. It all comes down to your gain on the sale.

TRAP

You cannot deduct a loss on a personal residence against your income taxes.

If you have a gain on the sale, you probably owe taxes on that gain, subject to the up-to-$500,000 exclusion for married couples filing jointly, discussed below. *Gain* is calculated as the difference between your adjusted basis and your *net selling price*. The actual calculation can be tricky and should be made by a tax specialist.

Much of the tax planning for a sale of a personal residence revolves around being sure that you qualify for the up-to-$500,000 exclusion (for married couples filing jointly) provided for under the 1997 Taxpayer Relief Act. According to this act, each person regardless of age can exclude up to $250,000 of the capital gain on a principal residence. For a married couple, that adds up to $500,000 when they file a joint return.

Obviously, being able to exclude up to $500,000 of the gain can make a huge difference in your tax liability. And for most people it's a highly desirable option. (I say "most" because for some wealthy taxpayers whose gain is substantially more than the maximum, there are other alternatives, such as converting to a rental and subsequently doing a tax-deferred exchange.)

How Do You Qualify for the Tax Exclusion?

There are some basic rules that must be followed in order to qualify for the exclusion.

Basic Rules for Qualifying for the Capital Gain Exclusion

- The home must be your principal residence—that is, you must own and occupy it.
- You must have lived in the property for two out of the previous five years.
- You can take the exclusion only once every two years.

While the basics are fairly simple, there are many circumstances that come close but do not quite fit the formula. Before considering these, however, let's take a quick look at what this law changed.

No Rollover Required

There were many tax planning rules prior to the change in the tax code, and unfortunately many people still think they apply. Here are some that are no longer applicable.

No Deferral Required. In the past, you had to purchase another property of the same or greater value in order to defer gain. At that time it was not an *exclusion* but a *deferral*. Your gain was deferred into the future and into the new property.

Today, that's no longer the case. You do not have to buy another property at any time nor defer the gain into it.

No Need to Buy Another Property. Further, the money that you take out of the property need not be reinvested in another property. You can do with it as you wish: take a holiday, gamble it away in Vegas, or give it to your children.

Eased Reporting. In the past the home sale had to be reported on Form 2119. That was eliminated a year after the new rules took effect. Generally speaking, if your gain does not exceed $250,000 per person or $500,000 per married couple filing jointly, you do not need to report the sale. If the gain exceeds these amounts, then you need to report it on Form 1040, Schedule D, to the federal government and as your state requires.

No Need to Move a Certain Number of Miles. You do not have to move a certain distance, for example, 50 miles, away from your old home in order to qualify for the exclusion.

No Age Requirement. In the past the rule applied only if you were age 55 or older. That provision has been repealed. You do not need to reach a minimum age in order to qualify.

No Once-in-a-Lifetime Provision. The fact that you previously took the exclusion under the old rules in no way precludes you from taking it again under the new rules. In effect, you get it back. However, you can take it only once every two years.

What Are the New Tax Exclusion Rules?

To qualify, the house must be your principal residence. That means that it must be your "main house." Often it means simply where you spend a majority of your time. If you have two houses (a second vacation home, for example), your principal residence is often determined by many factors including the following.

It's Your Principal Residence If . . .

- It's near where you work.
- It's where you and your family reside.
- It's where you are registered to vote.
- It's the address you use when sending in your federal and state tax returns, and it's your mailing address for bills.

There may be other evidence available to you to prove a property is your principal residence.

You must also live in it for a minimum of two out of five years. That means that if you moved in yesterday, it will be two years before you can claim the exclusion. (There are some extenuating circumstances, which we'll discuss shortly.)

From a tax planning standpoint, assuming you'll make a gain on the sale of your house, it's probably to your advantage to remain in the home at least two years before selling it.

Do You Have to Live There Continuously?

While you may plan on residing in your home right now, your circumstances may change in the future. You may find that you need to move away because of a job change, a change in your marital situation, a change in your health, or some other reason. Rather than sell the property, you may opt to rent it out. In such cases, renting it will not preclude claiming the exclusion provided that the required years lived in it are met.

Remember, you must have resided in the property for *two out of the previous five years*. (That's not three or one.) That means that you can rent the property out for three out of the previous five years. Furthermore, the periods of occupancy and renting do not have to be continuous. You could live in it for a year, rent it out for three years, and then come back and live in it for one year, and thus meet the requirement.

Extended Vacations?

It's okay to take temporary vacations. But the exclusion can be affected by certain circumstances. For example, if you take a cruise that lasts a month, it is undoubtedly a temporary vacation and shouldn't affect your occupancy status with regard to the home.

On the other hand, if you move to another country for 13 months, then it's a different story. Even if you don't rent the property out during that time, the IRS might consider your move other than "temporary."

Two Unmarried Owners?

Each one must independently qualify for the maximum limitation. Each will file a separate return and report the gains, and each may claim up to the $250,000 exclusion.

Only One Spouse Qualifies?

This opens a whole can of worms. For example, it is possible for each spouse to have his or her separate principal residence. If that's the case, then each could potentially qualify for the up-to-$250,000 exclusion on the properties, provided that they meet the basic requirements.

But if both spouses own the property but only one has occupied it for two years (as when there is a marriage and one member previously owned the house), then only the spouse who has occupied it for two years may claim the exclusion.

Are There Exceptions to the New Tax Exclusion Rules?

Even though you fully intend to meet the guidelines of the exclusion rule, circumstances may prevent you from doing so. If that's the case, then you may still be able to claim at least a part, if not all, of the amount.

Possible Exceptions to the Rule

- **Employment issues.** You might lose your current job and find another one far away. If the move is more than 50 miles, you might be forced to sell your home and could challenge the two-out-of-five-year rule.
- **Health issues.** You may contract an illness or have an accident that necessitates your moving from the house. Again, this is a situation in which you could challenge the rule.
- **Unforeseen issues.** Generally speaking you will need to establish that the primary reason for the sale was unanticipated.

What's important to understand is that the exceptions are handled on a case-by-case basis. Common exceptions cited in the past include condemnation of the house or break-up of a couple that intended to get married.

Don't Assume Anything, but Rather Check with a Good Tax Professional First

If you have a qualified exception, then you may get at least a partial exclusion. Generally speaking this is determined by one of two formulas. Either you divide the days of use into two years (730 days) or the days between the sale of your last home that qualified for the exclusion and the current sale into two years. Whichever is less is taken as a percentage that then applies to the up-to-$500,000 exclusion for a couple filing jointly. If, for example, you had a qualified exception, hadn't previously taken the exclusion (for two years), and you occupied your principal residence for six months, you would probably end up with one-fourth of the exclusion amount.

How Important Is Record Keeping?

Most people have no idea what their gain is going to be. Homes purchased as recently as just five years ago in some areas of the country have doubled and even tripled in value.

To be safe, you should keep records that will affect the tax basis of your property. Who knows, when it comes time to sell, you may find that your gain is more than the $250,000 for individuals or $500,000 limit for married couples filing jointly, and you would have tax to pay on the excess.

However, if you've got records of your home improvements, your basis could be adjusted upward. Then you may find you actually don't owe as much, or any at all.

Always keep good records.

Getting Started on a Budget — and over a Weekend!

So, you want to buy your own home?

There's no time better than the present to get started. But just what do you do to push off, to get your feet wet, to start the process?

It's actually quite easy. You can be up and running as a qualified buyer in less than a weekend. By the end of that weekend you may have picked your neighborhood and even have some specific homes you want to check out.

Here's how to get started.

Make a Budget

Presumably you want to use the same money you're paying as rent, to pay for your new home. However, you may find that you can afford to pay more . . . or less, monthly. You won't know, however, until you prepare a budget.

Preparing a home-buying budget is easy. You don't need to spend a lot of time doing it. You can prepare it in an hour one evening. Here's what I suggest you include.

Basic Budget to Determine How Much You Can Afford to Pay Monthly to Buy a Home

Income

Your salary	$_____	
Your spouse's salary	$_____	
Self-employment income	$_____	
All other income (alimony, interest, dividends, and so on)	$_____	
Total		$_____

Fixed Expenses

All utilities (water, TV, and so on)	$_____	
Automobile payments	$_____	
Automobile expenses (gas, oil, and so on)	$_____	
Credit card payments	$_____	
Other long-term debt	$_____	
Food and clothing	$_____	
Other household expenses	$_____	
Total		$_____
Available cash after all fixed expenses		$_____

Variable Expenses

Entertainment	$_____	
Travel	$_____	
Meals	$_____	
Clothing	$_____	
Medical	$_____	
Other variable expenses	$_____	
Total		$_____
Available cash after all fixed and variable expenses		$_____

Note that we end up with two figures for how much cash we have available after expenses. The first is a kind of bottom line—that's what you can afford to apply to rent if you give up a lot of desirables such as travel and entertainment. The second is what you have left if you don't change your lifestyle. What most people do is pick a figure somewhere between the two.

Get Preapproval

From the above budget, you'll quickly learn how much you feel you can spend each month on house payments. Now a lender needs to tell you how much it thinks you can afford.

You can get preapproval either from a physical lender, such as a mortgage broker or bank, or an Internet lender. In many cases, using electronic underwriting, this can be done in an hour or two. You'll typically fill out a form containing 60 or so questions. In a good preapproval (one that the lender should honor at the closing), your credit, bank balances, and employment will also be verified.

You fill out an application, get a credit report and score (see Chapters 6 and 7), and end up with a letter that tells you what you can afford each month and how big a mortgage that translates into. Factored into this should be the amount you have to put as a down payment and closing costs. You can take this letter to sellers to convince them that you'll qualify to purchase their home. However, the letter does not automatically mean you've gotten the mortgage. Before funding, the lender will want to be sure that the home appraises out, that any additional qualifying requirements are met, and that your financial condition hasn't changed.

Check the Timing

Many real estate agents will tell you that now is always a good time to buy. In many respects they're correct, as we saw in Chapters 1 and 2. It's hard to go wrong buying real estate for the long term at any time.

On the other hand, some times to buy are better than others. The best time is just as a slow market is ending and the real estate cycle is turning upward. The worst is just as a hot market is ending and the real estate cycle is turning downward.

You can determine where the market is in the real estate cycle by following the real estate and business sections of your local newspaper. Invariably the real estate market is news and the media will cover how it's doing. A few factual articles can quickly get you up to speed.

A better source is to check out the local inventory and median price. Both are available from local real estate boards through virtually any broker. A large and increasing inventory indicates a market that's slowing and suggests slowing price appreciation in the future. A small and decreasing inventory indicates just the opposite. Confirm this by looking at what's happened to the median price of homes in the area over the past year (also available online through brokers).

Know Your Determination

Ultimately you have to decide if you're a renter or an owner. For some, having the landlord be responsible for upkeep is comforting. When an appliance goes out, the toilet gets plugged, or the air-conditioning stops working, you just call the landlord and it's his or her problem, not yours. For several years I rented an apartment, and I found the lack of responsibility appealing.

(Of course, during that same period I owned several homes and found the price appreciation and gain in equity even more appealing!)

Most people prefer the security, independence, privacy, and of course potential profit that ownership offers. The question is, how determined are you to become an owner?

Getting a rental is easy. You just fill out the rental application and contract, pay a few months' rent, and move in.

Getting a home of your own is a bit more complicated. As noted above, you should create a budget and obtain a preapproval. Then you'll need to work with agents, look at properties, negotiate with sellers, and often spend a month or more closing the deal.

Buying a home requires determined effort. Are you willing to make it?

Yes, the rewards of ownership are plentiful. But they don't go to the lazy or to those who lack determination. You won't just fall into owning a home—you have to go out there and make it happen.

Get an Agent

You can find and buy a home entirely by yourself. But why would you want to do that when there are agents aplenty out there ready and eager to do all the legwork for you? Besides, in nearly all cases the seller pays the agent's fee, so to you, their services are free. Don't attempt to reinvent the wheel—go with the existing system and get an agent working for you.

As noted, there are lots of agents out there. But how do you find just the right agent who will do the best job for you?

The first step is to find agents in the area where you want to buy. You may not know your exact neighborhood, but you undoubtedly at least know the town or the area of the city where you want to live. Look for an agent in that area.

One of the most important criteria for selecting an agent is that he or she be *local*. Local agents know the neighborhoods, schools, shopping, transportation, and sellers. They can save you loads of time and usually can come up with the best deal.

How to Choose an Agent

Get referrals from friends and family whom you trust. Look for signs that indicate one agent is more active in the area than others. Check out the agent's Web site.

Once you narrow the field to several agents, conduct interviews. Think of it as hiring an employee.

Conducting the Interview

1. Make sure the agent is local. All real estate is local, so an agent who lives and works in the neighborhoods you're interested in will be best positioned to find the right home for you. Beware of working with an agent who's out of the territory, even out by just 10 miles. That agent likely won't know the local agents and probably won't know the properties very well.

2. Determine if the agent is experienced. The last thing you need is to get an agent who just got licensed and wants to learn on you. Yes, this agent may indeed be willing to take extra time on your account—mainly because he or she doesn't have any other clients! But you want an agent who's been around the block, who knows how to find properties and get offers accepted. Typically this means someone who's been in the field for at least five years. If you ask an agent you're interviewing how long he or she has been selling real estate, most won't hesitate to tell you.

3. Make sure the agent is active. In real estate it's not uncommon to find *inactive agents*. These are people who have a real estate license but don't actually make a living in the business. Instead, they may be on retirement from another career and are simply trying to earn a few bucks on the side selling property. There's nothing wrong with this. It's just that these part-timers often aren't on top of the market. And they may be hesitant about taking in offers and even about working with active agents. You want a full-time, active agent on your case.

It's okay if the agent doesn't devote his or her full time just to you. What you want, however, is an agent who devotes his or her full time to real estate. You want to avoid an agent who spends a couple of hours a week in the office and, as a result, doesn't really know the market or how to deal with sellers.

4. Be sure your agent can close. *Closing* means making the sale. Some deals can't be made, particularly when you're lowballing the seller. But *if* the deal can be made, you want to be sure that your agent can make it.

I recall one agent I knew who thought she was a hotshot. She would tell her buyer clients that if she couldn't get their offer accepted, no one could. However, when it was time to close the deal, when she was negotiating with the seller and his or her agent, she was a cream puff. She had no idea when to give and when to be firm, when to insist on a price and when to compromise. Hence, she only closed the easy deals.

Ask your agent how he or she will deal with a seller. See what they say. The answer can be instructive. An agent who can close will talk about such things as identifying objections and turning them around into positives; about sticking with it and wearing the sellers down; at some point, about giving an ultimatum "that they can't refuse"; and so on. In other words, an agent who can close will talk about closing.

In contrast, if your agent talks about being polite to the sellers, about giving them enough time to decide, about not making them angry so they'll reject your offer, consider getting another agent.

Although you probably won't discover it until well into a deal, a sure sign of an agent who can't close is when he or she insists that you must give the sellers plenty of time to decide on the offer, two or three days at least. This is a no-no. You never want to give the sellers lots of time. The sellers might talk themselves into and out of the offer during that time. Another, better offer might come in and squeeze yours out. The ability to use time to your advantage is one of the biggest assets a good agent has. You want your agent to say something like, "We'll give them till midnight tonight to decide," and it's 6 p.m. when he or she says it. This agent has the confidence in his or her ability to close the deal.

5. Make sure your agent is completely honest. Most agents are. But there is an occasional bad apple. A person's honesty is hard to determine until you've been around that person for a while, but there are a few clues to help you know either way. Watch out for misstatements. Exaggeration is one thing, but if an agent tells you something about a house that you later learn is totally untrue, it's time to move on. One tip-off that an agent may be dishonest is if he or she boasts about cheating or in some way deceiving another buyer or a seller. Sometimes the agent will say such a thing to imply that you're in good hands because he or she knows how it's done, but he or she would never do it to you. However, my experience is that an agent who cheats one person will have no scruples when it comes to cheating another, such as you. You want someone who goes out of his or her way to be sure that no one who's party to a deal is injured.

6. Make sure your agent is a member of local organizations. It almost goes without saying that your agent should be a Realtor, a member of the National Association of Realtors, the largest national trade organization. This should also entitle your agent to be a member of your local multiple listing service (MLS), which handles cobroker listings. These are listings that all the agents in the area work on. And your agent should be a member of the local real estate board, which often administers the MLS.

7. Get recommendations on your agent. If you don't know an agent, get someone to recommend one. A personal reference from a relative, friend, or coworker at least can set you in the right direction. Once you locate the agent, ask him or her to supply you with half a dozen recommendations of previously satisfied customers. (That should be easy to do for someone who's been in the business several years.) Then call several of them. Find out how long the agent worked with them. Were they "hot" buyers, or did they have afford-ability issues. The most important question to ask is, "Would you use this agent again?" Hopefully, they'll all say an unqualified, "Yes!"

8. When possible, work with a buyer's agent. A listing agent almost certainly represents the seller. You want an agent who looks out for your interests first. That's a buyer's agent. (Most buyer's agents get paid by splitting the commission with the seller's agent.) Ask the agent whom he or she represents. They have to tell you and put it in writing.

Note: Portions of this list first appeared in my book *How to Buy a Home When You Can't Afford It* (McGraw-Hill, 2002).

Working with Multiple Agents

You can work with several agents at one time, but just remember the Biblical injunction that what you sow, you shall reap. If you work with more than one agent at a time, you're showing a lack of loyalty.

As a consequence, don't expect any agent to be particularly loyal to you. When agents find that you're "playing the field," they may ignore you, not show you the best deals (saving those for their loyal clients), and in general give you less-than-perfect service.

My suggestion is that you work with one agent at a time. Be loyal to that agent until he or she demonstrates that he or she can't really help you. Then feel free to move on.

Narrow the Search

As noted, all real estate is local. After you've been looking for a few days, you'll quickly discover those neighborhoods in which you want to live and that you can afford. Then concentrate on finding just the right house in them.

Of course, you'll want a "good" neighborhood, and here's how to determine if the one you've selected is just that.

Features of a "Good" Neighborhood

- **Steady increase in valuations.** The properties over time have not only been maintained but have increased in value. Check sales in the area going back at least five years.
- **Good schools.** This is probably the single most important factor in a neighborhood's value. Check scholastic scores (available from the school district office). Ask local parents what they think of the schools. See if the area has passed school tax assessments. (Tax increases for schools are actually good things as they better the schools, which ultimately results in a better neighborhood.)

- **Low crime rate.** Statistics should be kept by the local police department. They often are specific not only to a neighborhood but right down to the block! Ask for the public affairs officer.
- **Good transportation.** Nearby mass transit is getting increasingly important as our cities "slow down" due to traffic congestion. Being nearby but not too close to a train and/or bus line is important. Having relatively close access to a freeway is also a plus.
- **Adequate shopping.** Though not critical since most people will travel up to 20 miles for shopping, it's important to have local stores for the basics such as groceries, hardware, and so on.
- **Employment opportunities.** Without jobs, no community can thrive. Be sure that the employment picture in the area in which you buy is healthy.

Make an Offer

Your agent will help you with this. (We covered it in some detail in Chapter 9.) The three most important things to remember are the following.

Most Important When Making an Offer

- **Know the value of the property.** You'll learn this by comparison shopping and also by getting a CMA.
- **Know how important the property is to you.** Try to leave your options open. If you feel you can always find another home, you'll be a better negotiator on this one.
- **Remember, it's only business.** Don't get angry at the seller or the agent . . . and always try to keep the negotiations moving forward.

Close the Deal and Move In!

It typically takes around 30 days to complete the purchase of the home. You and your agent need to do the following during this time:

Closing the Deal

- **Secure your financing.** Check with the lender who preapproved you as soon as possible. There may be other hoops to jump through before the lender will fund your money.
- **Approve the disclosures and inspection reports.** Get to this early on in case there are repairs to be made or renegotiations to handle.
- **Check on the sellers.** Make sure they are able to give a clear title.
- **Do a final walk-through.** Make sure the home is in the same condition as when you first saw it.
- **Sign the loan documents and close escrow.**

There's nothing quite as pleasurable as getting the keys to your new home. Finally, all the effort, time, and money seem worthwhile.

Once you're an owner, being a renter will seem like something from a dim and distant past. You may ask yourself why would you ever rent, when you can own?

Of course, now you know the answer to this question.

What You Should Know about ARMs

The best way to understand an ARM (adjustable-rate mortgage) is to compare it to a fixed-rate mortgage.

With a fixed-rate mortgage, you always know where you stand. Your interest rate and, hence, your monthly payment remain constant for the life of the loan whether it be for 3 years or 30 years.

With an ARM, it's quite different. Your interest rate fluctuates. It moves up and down depending on market conditions. Hence, your monthly payment, which reflects the interest rate, likewise can vary up or down over the life of the loan.

Some of the material in this appendix originally appeared in my book *How to Buy a Home When You Can't Afford It* (McGraw-Hill, 2002).

Low Initial Rate: The Teaser

Given a choice between a mortgage where you never know what your monthly payment is going to be and a mortgage where the monthly payment is fixed, any reasonable person would opt for the fixed-rate mortgage. It's a no-brainer.

Therefore, lenders have to sweeten the pot to entice borrowers to go for the ARM. The sweetener they use is the *teaser*. This is an artificially low initial interest rate and, hence, low initial monthly payment. The lender says, in effect, "If you take the ARM, I'll cut your monthly payments at the beginning." That's quite an inducement; indeed, it's what makes this loan so affordable.

TIP

The real key to deciding whether or not to get an ARM is knowing how much the teaser is and *how long* the teaser rate lasts. If you get an initial low rate and payment for just one month and then it goes up, you've hardly accomplished anything. On the other hand, if the low monthly payment lasts for several years, it can be just the right thing.

The Consumer's Strategy

The theory behind using an ARM for most consumers is twofold. First, you want the teaser to be as long as possible so you get a lower monthly payment than you otherwise would get. Second, you hope that once the teaser terminates and your interest rate and payment go up, you can refinance to another ARM with another low teaser (or, if interest rates have fallen, to a low fixed-rate and fixed-payment mortgage). Thus, at least in theory, you can keep on going almost indefinitely with a low monthly payment.

TRAP

Don't overlook the high transaction costs of refinancing. They can typically be between 2 and 5 percent of the mortgage. In recent years, however, lenders have been willing to roll these costs over into either a slightly higher interest rate or increased mortgage amount. Also, if you refinance with the same lender, very often these transaction costs can be dramatically reduced.

The Lender's Perspective

It's worthwhile to take a moment to understand why a lender would want you to use an ARM and would entice you to get one with a teaser. The reason has nothing to do with altruism.

The standard term of a real estate mortgage is 30 years, and that is a very long time. The problem for the lender is that over the course of those 30 years, interest rates can rise very high, particularly if there's an inflationary period.

When interest rates go up, mortgages with fixed low rates are worth less. (Mortgages operate just like bonds.) This adversely affects the lender's portfolio.

In order to reduce the risk of losing income from mortgages when interest rates are rising during inflationary times, lenders would like to be able to adjust the interest rates on their existing mortgages. They'd like to be able to raise the mortgage rates to reflect the higher market rates, thus protecting their portfolio. Hence, the concept of the ARM: the mortgage in which the lender can raise rates.

Thus, the ARM is basically a device to protect lenders, not borrowers. However, because no reasonable borrower would freely give a lender the additional power of raising rates (and monthly payments), lenders are forced to give borrowers something in return—the teaser.

All of the back and forth between lender and borrower usually centers on how big the interest rate reductions are and how long that teaser lasts. The lender wants it for as short a time as possible. The borrower wants it for as long as possible.

TIP

Be sure you check out lots of different ARMs. Each lender has its own policy on the teaser. While one may offer it for only three months, another may offer it for three years.

The Basics of an ARM

Having gone into the tactics used by both borrower and lender on an ARM, let's now turn to how these mortgages actually work in practice. It's a somewhat arcane process.

All ARMs have at least four things in common:

1. An index
2. A margin
3. An adjustment period
4. Steps

What Is an Index?

Since the interest rate (and monthly payment) of the ARM goes up and down, there must be some objective indicator to determine when and how much these fluctuations will be. (It wouldn't do to have the lender arbitrarily raise interest rates and payments at its whim!)

In order to determine what the interest rate for an ARM is, therefore, the mortgage is indexed. This means that the interest rate of the ARM is tied to some well-known economic measure that can't be influenced by the lender. Typical indexes include Treasury bill rates of various lengths, the cost of mortgage funds to the lender, and the cost of funds available to the borrower from government agencies.

The way the index works is quite simple. If the index falls, the ARM's interest rate will fall. If the index rises, the ARM's interest rate will rise.

TIP

Lenders usually want their ARMs tied to indexes that record volatility in the market. But borrowers usually want their ARMs tied to those indexes that tend to move slowly, if at all. Finding the right index is one of the important features when selecting an ARM.

Stability of the index means that interest rates and monthly payments aren't likely to fluctuate too much. A volatile index means that your payments could be all over the board. For most borrowers wide fluctuations in the monthly payment are very hard to handle.

The agencies that regulate ARMs do not specify which index a lender must use. Rather, it is up to the lender to make this selection. The regulators only specify that the index must be one over which the lender has no control, it must reflect interest rates in general, and it must be widely publicized.

Most Common Indexes

> Six-month Treasury
> One-year Treasury
> Three-year Treasury
> Cost of funds rate
> Average cost of fixed-rate mortgages
> LIBOR (London Interbank Offered Rate)

Treasury Securities Index. Published weekly by the Federal Reserve Board, this gives the constant maturity interest rate for Treasury securities. This is the interest rate that investors pay to buy these government debts.

Ten-Year History

Six-month T-bill. Most volatile of indexes; most closely reflects current market money conditions. Based on the weekly auction rates.

One-year T-bill. Also volatile. Based on the weekly average of daily yields of actively traded one-year T-bills.

Three- to five-year T-note. Similarly volatile. Based on constant maturities.

Cost of Funds Index. Compiled by the Federal Home Loan Bank Board (FHLBB), this gives the average interest rate that member banks and savings and loan associations paid during the previous period. It is reported monthly and by district. It represents the cost to members (banks and savings and loans) of money if they have to borrow from the government.

>   History. Stable, less dramatic movements up and down. Most commonly used is the 11th District Cost of Funds Index (COFI).

Average Cost of Fixed-Rate Mortgages. This index is composed of the average interest rate for newly originated fixed- and adjustable-rate conventional mortgages of previously occupied homes for major lenders. It is published monthly, and it is probably the most accurate assessment of mortgage interest changes.

>   History. Stable. One of the less volatile measures.

London Interbank Offered Rates Index. Almost no one outside of the lending industry has heard of the London Interbank Offered Rate (LIBOR) Index. Yet it is one of the oldest. It is also one of the most stable. If you can find a lender who uses this rate, and if the margin is not unreasonable, it might be one of the best to use.

>   History. Quite stable.

When a lender offers you an index, the lender is required by law to show you the history of the index going back several years. Just be sure that the index history covers the volatile interest rate period of 1978 to 1982. Those years will tell you more than any others about what this index is likely to do when interest rates skyrocket.

How Do You Pick an Index?

Obviously you can't pick an index. The lender does this. But you can shop for lenders until you find one that uses the index most suited to your needs.

You want to pick a lender who uses an index that shows some stability over time. But be careful. An index that is volatile, when it is down, may give you a better teaser rate and payment than an index that is stable but stays up.

TIP

Interest rates fluctuate up and down over time. The best time to get an ARM is when interest rates are high. That way, when they fall in the future, your payments are more likely to go down. The worst time to get an ARM is when interest rates are low. You are almost guaranteed higher payments as interest rates rise in the future.

What Is a Margin?

The interest rate you pay on your mortgage is not simply the interest rate that the index reflects. Rather, the lender will add a *margin* to the index to determine your actual mortgage interest rate.

For example, the lender may specify in your ARM documents that the margin is 3 percent. That means that when the index is 4 percent, for example, the lender adds the margin of 3 percent to the 4 percent, and you have an effective mortgage interest rate of 7 percent.

The margin is tied directly to the index used. If the index is generally low, the lender will tend to use a higher margin. If the index is generally high, the lender will tend to use a lower margin.

What Is an Adjustment Period?

After the index, the next critical feature to look at in an ARM is the adjustment period. How frequently can the lender adjust the mortgage rate up or down?

The adjustment period is arbitrary, and each lender will specify what it wants in the loan documents. Therefore, for the borrower this is something you can pick and choose only by switching lenders. Here are some of the more commonly used adjustment periods.

ARM Adjustment Periods

Monthly

Bimonthly

Every three months

Every six months

Annually

Biannually

Every three years

Every five years

To keep the teaser rate longer, you will usually want the longest adjustment period possible. This gives you the longest period of having low payments. However, lenders typically want the shortest adjustment periods. This gives them the greatest protection against interest rate hikes.

Therefore, when shopping for a mortgage, it is highly advisable to place the adjustment period as a big priority on the list of terms to look for.

What Is a Hybrid?

There are many *hybrid mortgages*. Some offer an adjustable rate for a few years, which can then be switched to a fixed rate. Some are "called" (become due) in seven years, even though they are amortized (the monthly payments are spread out) over 30 years. There are numerous variations, and all have their distinct advantages and problems, and we will discuss these at the end of this appendix.

What Are Steps?

Many ARMs set a maximum limit on the amount the interest can be raised each adjustment period. For example, some ARMs have a 1 or

2 percent interest rate adjustment. That means that regardless of the amount that the real interest rate has moved, the interest rate on the mortgage can be adjusted only in steps of 1 or 2 percent.

To see how steps work, let's say interest rates on our index have gone through the roof. Can an ARM interest rate in one adjustment period be raised to accommodate the full interest rate hike? If the original rate was 5 percent and interest rates spike by 5 percent, can the ARM's interest rate be raised by 5 percent (which would have the effect of almost doubling the monthly payment!)?

If the loan did not have steps, then the answer would be "Yes!" However, many ARMs have steps that limit the hikes in interest rate for each adjustment period. These limits are typically anywhere from 1/2 percent to 2 1/2 percent per adjustment period. Thus, regardless of what the index the mortgage is tied to may do, the interest rate cannot be hiked more than the step amount each period.

To get a better sense of how steps work, let's compare two different mortgages. The first has a step of 1 percent per adjustment period. The second has a step of 2 percent. Both mortgages have adjustment periods of six months.

With the first mortgage, when interest rates spike, after six months the interest rate on the mortgage goes up 1 percent, and after a year it goes up 2 percent.

With the second mortgage, when interest rates spike, after six months the interest rate on the mortgage goes up 2 percent, and after a year it goes up 4 percent.

The effect is that the increase on the monthly payment in the second mortgage is *twice* that of the first mortgage.

The point is that the smaller the steps, the greater the lag time accommodating a spike in interest rates. (Of course, a sudden decline would not be felt as quickly either.) The result is far more stability in the monthly payment. It also means that there's going to be a greater time during which the teaser rate is likely to continue in effect.

ARM lenders are concerned about the lag in mortgages with small steps. They see that they could lose out on interest during spikes in interest rates. Naturally enough, they want the mortgage interest rate to keep pace with the index, and they realize that mortgages with small steps would lag behind, thus causing them to lose interest income. As a consequence, many ARMs are written with *catch-up clauses*. These clauses provide that even though the step doesn't rise fast enough to keep pace with the index, any interest lost to the lender in this fashion will be carried over to the next adjustment period.

With a catch-up clause in a mortgage, the beneficial effects of smaller steps are nullified over a long period of time. In the previous example, the mortgage with 1 percent steps would continue to increase toward the maximum even after the index had turned down. It would continue on up until all the interest due to increases in the rate had been given to the lender.

TRAP

The answer for the borrower in a situation where there are large steps and/or catch-up clauses is to bail out of the mortgage and refinance. The one control the borrower has is to simply say, "Nope, I won't play this game anymore." The great danger, of course, is that your financial situation or the mortgage marketplace, or both, could change for the worse and you might not be able to refinance.

TIP

Although catch-up clauses tend to nullify the beneficial effect of smaller steps in the long run, they don't do so in the short run. If you plan to sell the property fairly quickly, small steps even with a catch-up clause can prove beneficial.

Interest Rate Caps

One of the biggest problems with ARMs is the uncertainty that they produce. The borrower never really knows what his or her payments are going to be tomorrow. It's this uncertainty that causes many borrowers to forgo ARMs.

Lenders are aware of borrowers' fears of hikes in mortgage payments caused by unlimited interest rate hikes on ARMs. If the mortgage were allowed to rise without restriction, in a very volatile market we might start out paying 7 percent and end up paying 15 percent or more. Our monthly payments could double as well! Few borrowers would take out a mortgage with such an unrestricted possibility.

To help reduce borrowers' fears, lenders frequently put an interest rate cap on the ARM. A *cap* is a limit on an ARM. It limits the amount the interest rate can rise (or fall). In this way the lender, appropriately, is assuming some of the risk for extremely volatile interest rate markets. (If there were a 6 percent cap—meaning that the interest rate on the ARM couldn't rise by more than 6 percent— and the market rate for interest rose by 10 percent, the lender would have to assume the loss of 4 percent in interest.)

The cap puts both a ceiling and a floor on the mortgage. The interest rate can't go above a certain amount. But it can't go below a certain amount either. If the cap is 5 percent, for example, the rate can rise above or fall below 5 percent of the current rate. But that amounts to a swing of 10 percent.

Note that mortgages with long teasers, say one to five years, often do *not* have caps. That means that at the end of the teaser period when the mortgage resets, the payments could shoot up.

A mortgage with a 3 percent cap is usually considered a far better mortgage than one with a 5 percent cap. And a mortgage with a 2 percent cap is better than the others. While this may seem obvious, it nevertheless is a consideration that should be taken.

Mortgage Payment Caps

In addition to setting a maximum cap on the interest rate of the mortgage, some ARMs also set a maximum limit on the amount the monthly payment can be raised each adjustment period, regardless of what happens to the interest rate.

A monthly payment cap states that the payment cannot rise beyond a certain percentage of the previous period's payment. A common payment cap is 7½ percent. The monthly payment in the new adjustment period cannot increase by more than 7½ percent of the payment in the preceding period.

To see how payment caps work, let's say interest rates on our index have gone through the roof. We have a maximum step of 2 percent per adjustment period. So the lender raises the interest rate a full 2 percent.

However, we also have a cap on the mortgage payment. It can't be raised more than, for example, 7½ percent each period. Here's what happens.

A Mortgage Payment Cap in Effect

The mortgage is $100,000 for 30 years with a payment cap of
   7½ percent (of the monthly payment).
The step for this mortgage is 2 percent.
If the required increase in the mortgage payment was $151 but
   the cap was 7½ percent of the mortgage payment, then the
   maximum increase in mortgage payment would be $66.

In other words, without the payment cap, the mortgage payment would rise $151. With it, the maximum rise is $66.

When interest rates rise dramatically, the monthly payment cap keeps the payment relatively stable. In the above example the payment cap kept the payment from rising by an additional $85.

For borrowers who have affordability issues and are scrimping to make the monthly payment, the payment cap seems a panacea. Get the payment cap and there's major protection. However, payment caps have a sinister side.

Negative Amortization

Negative amortization is something that is often hidden from view, unless you know what to look for in the mortgage documents. Although the negative amortization terms usually are fully explained in those mortgages in which it occurs, many people simply don't understand the implications. Many of us still fail to see the dangers.

Negative amortization means that instead of the amount we owe going down, it goes up! Each month instead of paying off some of the loan, we add to it. We end up owing more than we originally borrowed and/or having a longer borrowing period. What I feel is even worse, we end up paying interest on interest.

Negative amortization typically comes about because our payments are capped and the cap is lower than the interest rate rises. It also occurs in option mortgages where the payment is set artificially low and the unpaid interest is added to the loan.

Wanting such caps or artificially set low payments, as we've seen, is only natural. We want our monthly payment to be as small as possible. Another big concern is that the monthly payment not rise too swiftly. Typically we have limited ability to increase our income. We are afraid that sudden large monthly payment increases could cause us to lose our property. We are seeking *protection*. Unfortunately, an artificially low monthly payment or a monthly payment cap may give the illusion of protection, but not the actual thing.

TRAP

Remember that a monthly payment cap does not limit interest rate increases. What a monthly payment cap does is to restrict that portion of the interest rate increase that you immediately pay. The portion that you do not pay, however, does not go away. Rather, it is added to the mortgage.

The key to understanding payment caps is to remember that the portion of the interest rate that is not reflected in the increased monthly payment does not disappear. It is added to the mortgage.

Thus, you're not getting away without paying it. You're getting away without paying it *now*. You will pay it over the term of the loan.

Federal lender regulations usually prohibit negative amortization from increasing beyond 125 percent of the original mortgage balance. For example, if your original balance was $100,000, the maximum that negative amortization might increase the mortgage is to $125,000.

Often an argument used by lenders to justify the bad effects of negative amortization is that housing price increases will more than offset it. Yes, we might be adding to the mortgage amount, but our house will be worth more anyhow, so why worry?

The hollowness of this argument comes from the fact that, although prices will most likely increase, negative amortization has the effect of giving that equity increase not to the borrower-owner, but to the lender. You don't get more equity, you get more loan! And what if housing prices remain static or actually decrease, as has happened in recent years?

Should You Avoid Negative Amortization at All Costs?

No. It can be a necessary evil. With affordability issues, your desire may be to lower and control the monthly payment on your mortgage at all costs. You must keep it down. If this is your situation and you're aware of what's happening, then negative amortization can simply be the penalty you pay for those lower payments. The key is that you're aware of what's happening.

Be aware that mortgage payment caps are often a trade-off for other important benefits. A lender who offers a monthly payment cap as an inducement to a borrower often feels justified in asking for more restrictive terms in other areas. For example, such a lender may demand a prepayment penalty. If you pay off the mortgage early, it might cost you six months of interest! Since you will want the flexibility of getting out of the mortgage when the teaser rate is up, this could be a big drawback.

Prepayment Penalties

Should you avoid prepayment penalties? Yes, absolutely. Avoid them in mortgages. They do you no good. They are simply the lender's attempts to lock you in—to keep you from bailing out of the mortgage when the teaser rate is up.

Always ask if the loan has a prepayment penalty. Until a few years ago, almost none did. Now lenders are increasingly trying to slip this in. Beware of it!

Ultimately a mortgage with a monthly payment cap may be higher than a mortgage without it. Consider the following example prepared from material offered by the Federal Home Loan Bank Board. In this case various interest rate caps are given, and the monthly payment is shown over a period of 29 years. The chart assumes that interest rates start at 6 percent, then rise to 9 percent at year 5 and remain there. It also assumes that there is no interest rate cap on the mortgage.

Notice that the lower the monthly payment cap, the lower the monthly payments initially. But over the long run, the lower

Cap Rate Comparison Chart, $100,000 30-Year Mortgage

YEAR	INTEREST RATE	MONTHLY PAYMENT			
		7 PERCENT CAP	7½ PERCENT CAP	10 PERCENT CAP	NO CAP
1	6	$ 514	$514	$514	$514
2	7	540	552	565	572
3	7.5	567	594	622	630
4	8	595	638	684	689
5	9	625	686	753	748
6	9	656	738	753	748
10	9	797	800	753	748
15	9	1,018	800	753	748
20	9	1,112	800	753	748
25	9	1,112	800	753	748
29	9	1,112	800	753	748

the monthly payment cap, the higher the monthly payments become as the lender plays catch-up trying to recoup interest not received because of the payment cap. A 7½ percent cap, for example, will result after year 10 in this example in a payment of $800. Without the cap, the payment would have been only $748.

Monthly payment caps can mean lower monthly payments now but higher monthly payments later on if you hang onto the mortgage.

ARMs with Caps on Both the Monthly Payment and Interest Rate

Some lenders use this combination, and borrowers sometimes think that it is a significantly better loan. With the interest rate capped, the loan is indeed better for the borrower. But it is questionable as to how significant is the benefit when there is also a monthly payment cap.

To see why, look back at our previous example. Let's say that in addition to the monthly payment being capped, the interest rate was capped at a 3 percent maximum change with steps of 1½ percent a year. The chart would work out exactly the same! The interest rate cap would have no effect since the interest rate rose only to the maximum (from 6 percent in our example to 9 percent) and the increases were never beyond the 1½ percent steps.

Only if the interest rate cap were lower—in our example, less than 3 percent—would it act to mitigate the negative effects of a monthly payment cap (something very unlikely).

When a mortgage has both an interest rate cap and a monthly payment cap, you automatically should suspect that the interest rate cap is set higher than the monthly payment cap and that negative amortization could take place. The reason is simple: if this weren't the case, if the interest rate cap were set sufficiently low that no negative amortization could take place, then no monthly payment cap would be necessary.

Types of ARMs

The most common is the straight 30-year ARM. However, there are many hybrids. The most common goes by the name of *fixed/adjustable*, or by its term—*3/30, 5/30, 7/30,* or *10/30.*

In these mortgages you have a fixed rate for the first 3, 5, 7, or 10 years. Then the mortgage converts to an ARM at the then current interest rate for the balance of its 30-year term.

The purpose of this mortgage is to give you a more stable monthly payment combined with a slightly lower interest rate (and payment). The reason this is possible is that (from the lender's perspective) this is actually a 3-, 5-, 7-, or 10-year fixed-rate loan. This relatively short term affords the lender less risk over time than a standard 30-year payback, and thus, you get a lower interest rate and payment. Typically, the shorter the initial fixed-rate term, the lower the interest rate and monthly payment. After the fixed-rate period, the loan reverts to a rather ugly ARM, and the lender assumes that you will refinance.

TRAP

Some of these loans don't have the ARM at the end. You owe the entire unpaid balance at the end of the 3-, 5-, 7-, or 10-year period! This is a no-no for you as you never can know what your financial situation will be in the future. Without the automatic ARM attached (no qualifying, the loan simply rolls over), you might find yourself unable to refinance. Your choices would then be to quickly sell or lose the property to foreclosure!

Convertible Option Mortgages

A *convertible option mortgage* is a loan with two different modes. The convertible blends adjustable- and fixed-rate features. You can get the big advantage of the adjustable-rate mortgage—that is, the lower initial interest rate—but you can also achieve increased stability over the life of the mortgage. For the lender, the convertible is a compromise. It doesn't lock the lender into a long-term fixed rate. On the other hand, it doesn't give the lender quite as much protection against volatility as the straight adjustable-rate mortgage.

A convertible mortgage is really like the fixed/adjustable mortgage we just discussed, only in reverse. You start out with an adjustable-rate mortgage. Then after a set number of years, you are given the option of converting to a fixed-rate mortgage (at then market rates).

For example, you might have an adjustable-rate mortgage with a low initial rate. It would be like any other ARM except that at, perhaps, year 3, at your option, you could convert it to a fixed-rate mortgage at the then current market rate.

TRAP

Some mortgages offer you this option for free. Others have a *conversion fee*. Obviously the mortgage without the conversion fee is better from your perspective.

The big advantage of a convertible remains that it's another way to get a lower interest rate and thus, a lower monthly payment. The lender gives you a lower rate because the mortgage is adjustable. Yet you get the opportunity to convert to a fixed-rate mortgage later on. Most lenders offer convertible mortgages of one sort or another.

If you get a convertible, be sure you're very clear on when the conversion occurs. You may have a very small window of opportunity, say, three months, to opt to convert to a fixed rate. If interest rates are high during that period, you would probably just pass. But if interest rates take a dip, that would be a most opportune time to exercise your option.

The value to you of a convertible loan comes from your ability to convert it to a fixed rate at some time in the future. If the conversion window happens to be during a period of lower interest rates, you can get into a fixed-rate mortgage for very little in costs.

Other Mortgages

The types of mortgages available are limited only by the imagination. Each lender may offer dozens, sometimes hundreds! Be sure to check with several lenders and you may find just the option you're looking for.

Index

About the Author

ROBERT IRWIN is one of America's foremost experts in every area of real estate. He is the author of McGraw-Hill's bestselling Tips and Traps series, as well as *The Home Buyer's Checklist, How to Get Started in Real Estate Investing, and How to Buy a Home When You Can't Afford It.* His books have sold more than one million copies. Visit his Web site at www.robertirwin.com.